MASTE

TIME

MASTER YOUR

LIFE

MASTER YOUR
TIME
MASTER YOUR
LIFE

The Breakthrough System to
Get More Results, Faster, in
Every Area of Your Life

BRIAN TRACY

A TarcherPerigee Book

tarcherperigee

An imprint of Penguin Random House LLC
375 Hudson Street
New York, New York 10014

First trade paperback edition 2017

TarcherPerigee with tp colophon is a registered
trademark of Penguin Random House LLC.

Most TarcherPerigee books are available at special quantity discounts for
bulk purchase for sales promotions, premiums, fund-raising, and educational
needs. Special books or book excerpts also can be created to fit specific
needs. For details, write: SpecialMarkets@penguinrandomhouse.com.

The Library of Congress has cataloged the hardcover edition as follows:

Names: Tracy, Brian, author.
Title: Master your time, master your life : the breakthrough system to get
more results, faster, in every area of your life / Brian Tracy.
Description: First edition. | New York, NY : TarcherPerigee, 2016.
Identifiers: LCCN 2016021429 | ISBN 9780399183812 (hardback)
Subjects: LCSH: Self-actualization (Psychology) | Time management. | Success.
| BISAC: SELF-HELP / Personal Growth / Success. | SELF-HELP / Time
Management.
Classification: LCC BF637.S4 T7297 2016 | DDC 650.1—dc23
ISBN 978-0-399-18382-9 (paperback)

Printed in the United States of America
ScoutAutomatedPrintCode

Book design by Pauline Neuwirth

CONTENTS

MASTER YOUR TIME

MASTER YOUR LIFE

DIFFERENT KINDS OF TIME

Do ye value life? Then waste not
time, for that is the stuff out of
which life is made.

—BENJAMIN FRANKLIN

This is a great time to be alive. There have never been more opportunities to do more things and to achieve more of your goals in all of human history than there are today.

You can live longer and better today than any other generation before you. Modern advances in medicine and healthcare are enabling more people to live to age eighty or ninety—or even one hundred—than ever imagined possible.

But with all these great opportunities for success, prosperity, long life, and happiness, you are probably feeling like most people: too much to do and too little time.

Because of the explosive growth of information, technology, and competition, the rate of change has accelerated almost beyond your capacity to keep up with it.

Today we need a new way to think about time, especially the different times of your life.

We find that each activity and responsibility in your life requires you to take a different approach to time if you want to get the best results from everything you do.

You need one kind of time for setting goals and deciding what you really want in life and another type of time for setting priorities, focusing on high-value tasks, and getting things done.

You need one type of time for interacting, communicating, negotiating, and administrating and another type of time at home with your family and your most important relationships.

The different types of time are often like oil and water; they don't mix very well together.

Any attempt to use the wrong type of time in the wrong area for it will lead to frustration, failure, and ineffectiveness.

THE QUALITY OF YOUR LIFE

The quality of your life is largely determined by the quality of your time management. But time management is really personal management, life management. It is management of yourself. If you don't control your time properly, it is difficult for you to control anything else.

Fortunately, the richest, most successful person in the world has the same twenty-four hours per day that you have. The difference between successful people and unsuccessful people is that successful people, sometimes with less potential and fewer opportunities, often accomplish vastly more than others because they use their time in a better and more effective way.

Your highest paid, most important skill is your ability to *think*, both before you act and while you are acting. It is your ability to choose what is more important and what is less important.

Psychologists tell us that your level of *self-esteem*—how much you like and respect yourself—is the key measure of how happy you are in any area of your life. The key to high self-esteem is a feeling of *self-efficacy*—the confidence that you can master your life, achieve your goals, perform your tasks, and get the results that are expected of you and that you expect from yourself.

Your most valuable financial asset is your *earning ability*. This is your ability to get results that people will pay you for. This again is largely determined by how you use your time when you are working and before and after your work.

Thomas Edison once wrote, "Thinking is the hardest work there is, which is why most people would rather die than think."

The way you think about time and the various possible ways you can use your time largely determine your effectiveness and the quality of every part of your life.

STOP AND THINK

Most people live in a *reactive-responsive mode*. When something happens around them, they react and respond immediately, automatically, unthinkingly, becoming slaves to the moment or to the latest ring on their smartphone or computer.

The key to taking full control over your time and your life is for you to *stop and think* before you react and respond. It is for you to identify the kind of time and behavior that is required of you at each moment, and then for you to respond appropriately to that situation.

British historian Arnold Toynbee won the Nobel Prize for his masterful twelve-volume work, *A Study of History*. This series of books traces the rise and fall of twenty-three great civilizations or empires over twenty-five hundred years. Toynbee found that there was a predictable cycle that an empire would go through, from its early beginnings through to its collapse.

Toynbee proposed the idea of the "challenge and

response theory of history." He showed that each great civilization started small, sometimes as a single tribe or village, and by repeatedly responding effectively to external challenges, usually from warring tribes and other human enemies, the group continued to grow and expand until it dominated large land masses.

The Mongol Empire, for example, the largest land empire in history, started with three people—Temüjin; his mother, Hoelun; and his young brother—after another Mongol tribe had wiped out their village. From that humble beginning, Temüjin, who later became known as Genghis Khan, "The Perfect Warrior," spread the Mongol Empire from the Sea of Japan across China, India, much of Russia, and the Middle East, all the way to the Mediterranean and the Danube.

YOUR CHOICES AND DECISIONS ARE EVERYTHING
■

It is the same with you and your life. As long as you respond effectively to the continuous challenges of daily life and work, you continue to grow smarter and more capable and move toward the fulfillment of your full potential.

More than anything, your success in both the short and the long term is largely determined by the way you respond to the inevitable and unavoidable difficulties and challenges of daily life. This is called your *response ability*, your ability to respond effectively to the non-stop and conflicting demands on your time.

In this book, you will learn a series of the best time usage and time management principles ever discovered, the same time management techniques and strategies practiced by the most successful and happy people in our society.

By practicing these methods and techniques, you will take full control over your time and your life, and achieve more in the next year or two than most people accomplish in several years or even in a lifetime.

When you become more thoughtful about your current situation and learn the most effective way to deal with different events, at different times, with different approaches, you will think with greater clarity and will respond with greater confidence than ever before.

STRATEGIC PLANNING AND GOAL SETTING TIME

There is one quality that one must

possess to win, and that is

definiteness of purpose, the

knowledge of what one wants and

a burning desire to achieve it.

—NAPOLEON HILL

One of the most important types of time is the time you spend thinking, deciding, and planning how to achieve the things you really want in life.

The biggest single waste of time is setting off without clear, specific goals. Many people waste their most productive years responding and reacting to whatever is going on around them and working to achieve the goals of other people instead of taking the time to become absolutely clear about what it is that they really want for themselves.

There is a saying: "Before you do anything, you have to do something else first."

Before you set off on the great adventure of life, you have to decide where you want to end up. The good news is there have never been more opportunities to achieve your goals than there are today. But only you can decide what you want.

What is the difference between the rich and the

poor? One explanation is that about 85 percent of wealthy people have one big goal they work on all the time. Only 3 percent of poor people have one big goal, and they work on it occasionally, if at all.

THE I PERCENT VERSUS THE 99 PERCENT

Today, there is great controversy over the difference between the 1 percenters and the rest of us. The claim is that the 1 percenters own or control more wealth than everyone else put together. However, that statistic is inaccurate.

The real difference is actually between the top 3 percent and the other 97 percent. Because most people start off with little or nothing, the real question ought to be, "How did the 3 percent, who started with nothing, become so successful in the course of one or two generations?"

The answer is simple. The top 3 percent have clear, written goals and plans that they work on every day. They know exactly who they are, what they want, and where they are going. They have a blueprint, a road map, that guides them faster and with ever-greater accuracy toward achieving the health, happiness, wealth, and prosperity that most people strive for all their lives.

As a result of having clear, written goals, they waste far less time than the average person. People with written goals and plans earn and accumulate, on average, ten times as much as other people with the same levels of intelligence and education.

CLARITY IS EVERYTHING
∎

There is a story of a hunter who goes to the edge of the woods, closes his eyes, and shoots his rifle into the forest. He then turns to his friend and says, "I sure hope something good runs into that!"

That is how too many people live their lives. They throw themselves at life, like a dog chasing a passing car, seldom catching anything. Most people go through their lives without goals, doing the best they can and just hoping something good will happen to them. But hope is not a strategy. It is a recipe for failure, if not disaster.

For you to maximize your time, to enjoy the greatest quantity and quality of riches and rewards, you need to take time regularly to think about your goals, especially when you're experiencing turbulence and rapid change. You need to become intensely goal oriented. Setting goals, making plans, and organizing your life around the things you really want to do and have are the greatest time management tools of all.

Goal setting and personal strategic planning require that you step back and take some time off, away from interruptions and distractions. You then answer several key questions to ensure that what you are doing on the outside is consistent with the person you are on the inside and in harmony with what you really want to achieve.

LOOK INTO YOURSELF
■

The first question you ask is, Who am I? Your answer to this question reveals your self-image, the person you think you are. Because your outer behaviors are always consistent with the way you see or describe yourself on the inside, this answer tells you a lot about yourself.

The sign over the Temple of Apollo at Delphi in Ancient Greece read, "Man, know thyself." This is the starting point of wisdom.

Socrates said, "The unexamined life is not worth living." Unless you carve out time regularly to examine your life and make sure that you are clear about your goals, and that they have not changed, you will become reactive-responsive, acting impulsively and often doing what other people want you to do.

Begin this goals analysis by realizing that you are unique, and potentially *extraordinary*. There has never been, nor ever will be, anyone exactly like you: Be yourself. Everyone else is already taken.

You are a special and complex combination of knowledge, experience, education, talents, abilities, interests, emotions, desires, and fears. In addition, from infancy onward, you have had a complex series of experiences that have shaped you into the person you are today.

You have special strengths and abilities and have been born with the capacity to be absolutely excellent at something, and maybe several things. Your great responsibility to yourself, and to others, is to find that special mission that you have been put on this earth to accomplish. You must clarify your vision, your life's purpose, your heart's desire.

DO WHAT YOU REALLY LOVE
∎

One of your great jobs in life is to find something you really love to do and then to put your whole heart into becoming absolutely excellent at doing that one thing.

Throughout your adult life and career, you need to ask and answer a series of questions. Your answers will change over time and with experience. You must be clear about your answers each time you address these questions and must be willing to change your responses as you get more information.

Begin by assuming that you have no limitations. Imagine that you could wave a magic wand and make your life ideal in every way. Ask yourself:

1. What do I *really* want to do with my life?
2. What do I *really, really* want to do with my life?
3. What do I *really, really, really* want to do with my life?

The third time you ask this question, with "really, really, really," is the key. It forces you to dig deep into yourself, moving past the superficial answers regarding money and success, and often gives you the answer you have been seeking. This is how you begin to unlock your full potential.

PERSONAL STRATEGIC PLANNING

Successful companies invest a lot of time and money developing strategic plans for their businesses. These are the carefully thought-out goals and plans they use to achieve greater success and profitability in competitive markets.

You need a strategic plan as well, a *personal* strategic plan, to ensure you accomplish the very most in the shortest period of time, making the fewest possible mistakes along the way.

Personal strategic planning focuses on four basic questions, which you should ask regularly:

1. *Where am I now in my life?* What have you accomplished so far? How much are you worth financially? What kind of family life do you have? What is your level of health and fitness?

2. *How did I get to where I am today?* What were the choices and decisions you made in the past to create your present life? What has been most responsible for your success to date? What has been the reason for your setbacks?

3. *Where do I want to go in the future?* Idealize and imagine a perfect future. Project forward five years and imagine that your life is excellent in every way. What would it look like? How would it be different from your life today?

4. *How can I get from where I am to where I want to be?* What are all the different things that you could do, starting today, to create your perfect future?

Clarity is your best friend. Personal strategic planning requires, first, that you set clear, written goals and, second, that you carefully examine the various strategies you can implement to achieve them.

Most people want to earn a lot of money doing something they enjoy and ultimately achieve financial independence. But only a small percentage of people will achieve this common goal. Why is this?

FIRST-GENERATION WEALTH
■

There are more than ten million millionaires in the United States alone, and more than 80 percent of them are self-made. In the world, there are almost two thousand billionaires, about 66 percent of whom are self-made as well. These are all individuals who started with nothing and achieved their financial success in one working lifetime, if not sooner. Why not you?

There are many different ways for you to achieve

your goals of high income, financial independence, or even wealth.

One high road to financial success is entrepreneurship, the ability to start and build your own successful business. Today, it is easier to start a business and get started offering a product or service than ever before. It takes less than twenty-four hours for you to register your business, set up a website, and start operating.

Many people become financially independent by specializing and becoming absolutely excellent in their fields, working for another company, and being paid very well. They go to work for someone else and work their way up, earning more and more over the years.

Fully 10 percent of millionaires are professionals, such as doctors, lawyers, architects, accountants, and engineers. They worked very hard for a long time, did excellent work, got great reputations, and were eventually paid very well.

You can choose the path of entrepreneurship and business building or you can choose to work for another company, especially a company with great potential that is just getting started. You can specialize and become excellent at what you do. You can be a big success in many different ways.

LISTEN TO YOURSELF

■

You can choose among different paths, depending on your personality, skills, temperament, and what you really enjoy. The good news is there is no single best way. Millions of people do very well financially working for someone else or by specializing or both. Others become successful in business or as entrepreneurs by mastering a wide variety of skills. Some do several things. They start their own businesses and then specialize at becoming very good performing a service or developing a product that people really want and are willing to pay for.

Clarity is probably 95 percent of success. The greater clarity you have about who you are and what you want, the easier it is for you to succeed under almost any condition or circumstances.

Thomas Carlyle wrote, "The man with no goals makes little progress on the smoothest road, whereas the man with clear goals makes progress on even the roughest road."

When you take the time to stop and think about what you really want and how to get it, you can save yourself years of hard work going back and forth making little progress. Forget about the mistakes of the past and focus on the future. There is a Turkish proverb that says, "No matter how long you have gone down the wrong road, turn back."

THE INTELLIGENCE FACTOR
■

Josh Billings, the western humorist, once said, "It ain't what a man knows what hurts him; it's what he knows that ain't true."

When I was growing up, my teachers and parents told me over and over that if I didn't get good grades, if I didn't graduate from high school, if I didn't go to college, I wouldn't be successful in life. And I believed them. When I failed out of high school, I resigned myself to a life of laboring jobs. For the next few years, I washed dishes, dug wells, worked in sawmills and factories, and sometimes slept in my car.

Finally, in frustration at seeing all the successful people around me, many younger than I, I began to challenge my beliefs about success and failure. I began to ask, "Why is it that some people are more successful than others?"

What I found out surprised me. I found that there was only a small relationship between success and high education, intelligence, good grades, coming from a wealthy family, or even natural ability.

Intelligence has been identified as an important quality of successful people in every field. But extensive research has found that many successful people did not have exceptional IQs, nor did they get great grades at school. They may have been above average in intelligence, but they were not geniuses.

A WAY OF ACTING

■

The experts have concluded that intelligence is more "a way of acting" than it is a matter of good grades or a high IQ. So what then is an intelligent way of acting? The answer is simple: You are acting *intelligently* when you are doing something that moves you toward one of the goals you have set for yourself. You are acting *unintelligently* whenever you do anything that is not moving you toward something you want.

In my seminars, I teach a simple technique that I promise will double the income of everyone in the room. I call this the A/B Method.

Here is how it works: You divide all your tasks and activities into two categories, A tasks and B tasks. A tasks are those activities that move you closer to the goals that you say you really want to accomplish. These are goals such as to be more successful in your field, to earn more money, to spend more time with your family and friends, and to enjoy excellent health.

B activities, on the other hand, are those that do not move you toward these goals or, even worse, move you away from them.

Here is a life-changing rule: *Do only A tasks.*

Discipline yourself to do only those tasks that enrich and enhance your life and work and that give you a feeling of forward motion toward achieving the things you want and becoming the kind of person you want to be.

This simple strategy will enable you to double and triple your productivity, performance, and results in the months and years ahead.

Best of all, when you are working on your most important goals, you will experience a winning feeling, a feeling of forward progress, of being happier and more fulfilled. Your self-esteem will go up. You will enjoy higher levels of self-respect and personal pride.

Even more, when you are working on and completing your most important tasks and goals, you earn the respect, esteem, and admiration of everyone around you. You quickly become one of the most valuable people in your organization.

THE GOAL SETTING AND ACHIEVING FORMULA

•

There is a simple yet powerful seven-step goal achieving formula, or recipe, that you can learn and practice for the rest of your life. I have taught this formula to more than one million people all over the United States and Canada, and in seventy-two other countries. Over the years, countless people have come up to me or e-mailed, saying almost the same words, over and over: "You changed my life; you made me rich." And it was always the goals.

STEP I: Decide exactly what you want. Most people never do this. Be specific. Your goals should be so clear that you could explain them to a six-year-old child, and a six-year-old child could turn around and explain them to another six-year-old child. In addition, the child should be able to tell you how close you are to your goals because they are so clear and simple.

One of the biggest mistakes people make is to think that they *already* have goals, when all they really have are hopes and dreams. As an exercise, when I ask my audiences if they have goals, they all raise their hands and say yes.

Then I ask them to give me some examples of their goals. They shout out things like "I want to be happy," or "I want to be rich," or "I want to travel," or "I want to have a nice family life."

But these are not goals. They are wishes and hopes common to all humankind. They are fantasies and dreams that everyone has. They are not clear, specific goals that you can focus on achieving every day. They cannot be measured. No one can tell you how close you are to achieving them.

PUT IT IN WRITING
■

STEP 2: Write it down. Only 3 percent of adults have written goals, and it seems that everyone else works for them. They earn, on average, ten times as much as people without written goals. Once you have written down your goal, make it measurable. Attach a number to it so that someone else can tell you how close you are to achieving it.

There is a rule that says, If you want to be successful, put a measure on every goal and activity; but if you want to be rich, put a *financial* measure on every goal and activity.

A recent management study that looked at the work of 150 scholars who studied thousands of companies in more than twenty countries found there were three factors that accounted for more than 80 percent of business success: clear goals and objectives, clear measures, and clear deadlines.

Remember, you can't hit a target you can't see. When you have clear goals and you can measure your progress, you will move ahead further and faster than if you don't.

WHEN DO YOU WANT IT?
■

STEP 3: Set a deadline. Decide exactly when you want to achieve a particular goal. If it is a longer-term goal, break it down into years, months, weeks, and even days. Some of the most successful people I know will break a ten-year goal into five-year goals, one-year goals, one-month goals, all the way down to daily activities. They then discipline themselves to complete one or more of those activities every day.

What if you don't achieve your goal by the initial deadline that you set? Simple: Set a new deadline, and then another, and another, and another, if necessary. When you set your first deadline, it will be based on the information you have at that time. But external factors can change. There can be a decline in the economy overall or something like a collapse of oil prices that changes everything in your business or industry. When something happens to throw you off your timetable, you set a new deadline. There are no unreasonable goals; only unreasonable deadlines.

THINK ON PAPER
■

STEP 4: Make a list of everything that you can think of that you can possibly do to achieve the goal. As you think of new things you can do or learn or people whom you could talk to, write them on your list. Keep writing until you can't think of anything else.

STEP 5: Organize your list by *sequence*. Create a checklist, ordering your tasks starting with what you have to do first to achieve your goal, then to what you have to do second, and all the way down to the final step you will need to take to achieve that goal.

You can also organize your list by *priority*. What is the most important item on your list? What is the second most important item? Practice the *80/20 Rule*, which says that 80 percent of your success will be determined by 20 percent of the things that you do. Often the most valuable and important thing you do in life, which can account for 80 percent of your success, is deciding on a goal and making a plan to achieve it in the first place.

A list of activities, organized by sequence and priority, becomes a *plan*. When you have a written goal and a plan, you move ahead of 97 percent of adults working today. You will begin to achieve much more success, faster, than ever before. The people around you will often be amazed.

BECOME ACTION ORIENTED
■

STEP 6: Take action on your plan. Do something. Do anything. But get going. Take the first step. And the good news is that you can always see the first step. You always know what to do to get started.

When you take the first step toward your goal, which is often the hardest step of all, you receive three great benefits. First, you will get immediate feedback, which will enable you to change your course or direction, if needed. Second, you will get more ideas on how to take additional and better actions to achieve your goal. Third, you will feel a surge of self-confidence and self-esteem. You will feel more powerful and in greater control of your life. You get all three of these benefits from the simple act of taking action, of taking the first step, toward your goal.

STEP 7: This step may be the most important step of all. It will revolutionize your life and in a very short time. It is simply this: Do something every day that moves you toward your most important goal. Seven days a week, 365 days a year, do something, small or large, that moves you one step forward toward your goal.

When you do something every day, you activate what is called the *Momentum Principle of Success*. This principle, based on Sir Isaac Newton's law of inertia, says that it takes an enormous amount of energy to get a body into motion in the first place, but it takes much less energy to keep that body moving forward. Just think about pushing a car from a dead stop. It takes tremendous effort to get the car moving forward, but then it takes less and less effort to keep the car moving forward, faster and faster. It's the same with you.

GOAL-SETTING EXERCISE

Now, take a clean sheet of paper. Write the word *Goals* and today's date at the top of the page. Then write down at least ten goals you would like to accomplish in the next twelve months or so. These can be one-day goals, one-week goals, one-month goals, six-month goals, and/or one-year goals. But they are all goals that you would like to achieve within the next year.

Write your goals in a special way that makes them more acceptable to your subconscious mind, your mental powerhouse. Write them using *the three P's*: personal, positive, and present tense.

Begin each goal with the word *I*. Your subconscious mind can work on a goal only if you tell it that it is *you* personally who wants this goal. For example, you could say, "I earn this specific amount of money by December 31 of this year."

Make your goals *positive*. Instead of saying "I don't smoke anymore," you say, "I am a nonsmoker." Your subconscious mind can accept commands that are phrased only in the positive voice.

Write your goals in the present tense. Your subconscious mind cannot relate to the past or the future. You therefore state your goal as though it were *already* a reality, as though you had already achieved it and you are describing your accomplishment to someone else.

Instead of saying, "I will earn a specific amount of money this year," you say, "I earn this specific amount of money by this specific date."

For example, you could say, "I drive a brand-new four-door BMW sedan by December 31 of this year."

Your subconscious mind then takes this command as an order and begins to work on it twenty-four hours a day. From the day you become clear about the goals you want to achieve and when you want to achieve them, and write them down, you will begin to receive a steady stream of ideas and insights that will help you move quickly toward your goal and will cause your goal to move faster toward you.

MAJOR DEFINITE PURPOSE

Napoleon Hill wrote, after twenty-two years of research into the wealthiest people in America, that all great success began with a "major definite purpose." This is the one goal that is more important to you than any other single goal. It is the one goal that can help you more to achieve more of your other goals than any single achievement.

Look at your list of ten goals and ask this question: If I could achieve any one goal on this list, within twenty-four hours, which one goal would have the *greatest positive impact on my life?*

Usually, this goal will jump out at you from the page. It is the one goal that excites you and motivates you more than anything else. It is the one goal that would make you happier than anything else if you were to achieve it. Whatever it is, put a circle around that goal.

Then take a clean sheet of paper and at the top write the words *I achieve this goal by this date*. This puts your goal into the three P's formula and adds a deadline.

Below these words, make a list of everything you can think of that you could do to achieve that goal. As you think of new items, add them to your list.

Next, organize your list into a plan, or blueprint. Determine what you need to do first, what you need to do second, and third, and so on.

Then take action on your list. Take the first step. Move out of your comfort zone and begin your journey toward achieving the one goal that could have the greatest positive difference in your life.

Finally, resolve to do something every day that moves you at least one step closer to your most important goal.

THE MILLIONAIRE MAKER
▪

We could call this the *Millionaire Maker Formula*. More people have achieved more success all over the world with this simple formula than any other method that has ever been taught or practiced.

Because *you become what you think about most of the time,* every morning when you wake up, think about your major definite purpose, your one big goal. As you go through the day, think about your goal. At the end of the day, think about your goal and review the progress you have made toward achieving it.

The more you think about your goal, the more you activate the *Law of Attraction.* You begin attracting ideas, people, money, and resources into your life that help you to move toward your goals faster and faster.

And something else happens. As you begin to make progress on your most important goal, you will find yourself making progress on many of your other goals at the same time. Every part of your life begins to improve. Your self-esteem and self-confidence go up. You feel more powerful and capable of achieving the things you want in life. You will persist longer and never give up. Eventually, you become unstoppable.

<<< ACTION EXERCISES >>>

1. Write down ten goals you want to achieve in the next twelve months.
2. Select the one goal that can have the greatest positive impact on your life and put a circle around it.
3. Make a written plan to achieve this goal by following the goal setting and achieving formula outlined in this chapter.

2

PRODUCTIVE TIME— GETTING MORE DONE

He who every morning plans the

transactions of the day and follows

out that plan, carries a thread that

will guide him through the

labyrinth of the most busy life.

—VICTOR HUGO

To perform at your best, you need to think about productivity in a different way from most people working today. Your ability to use your working time well, to be highly productive, and to get more done faster and of better quality will have more of an effect on your career than any other factor. Productivity is achieved when you plan, organize, set priorities, and concentrate on the most valuable use of your time, all day long.

Productive work requires high levels of mental and physical energy, discipline, focus, and determination to get the job done quickly and well.

The way you think about your work will largely determine how much of it you do and how well you do it. The three most important words in thinking about personal productivity are *clarity*, *focus*, and *concentration*.

The first keyword is *clarity*. The starting point of developing greater clarity, which accounts for as much as 95 percent of your success, is for you to continually ask and answer this question: What results are expected of me?

In life and work, results are everything. They are the major if not the sole determinate of your income, your reputation, your future, and the way people both think and talk about you.

Successful people at work are described by others as being "highly productive." They develop a reputation for being "results oriented." They become the "go-to people" whenever anyone needs something big and important to be done, done well, and done on time. Your goal is to be one of those people.

YOUR PERSONAL BRAND

■

Each person has a "brand" in the minds of other people. This is usually summarized in a few words that others use when they think about you and describe you to others. Your personal brand largely determines much of what happens to you in life and work.

Recent research shows that when you meet a new person, you look for two sets of qualities that make up their personal brand. The first qualities are "warmth and trust." Is this a likable person whom you can trust and be comfortable with? Interestingly enough, you make this decision about another person within five seconds of meeting them for the first time. And you are seldom wrong.

The second quality people look for is a combination of "competence and ability." Can this person and will this person do the job in an excellent and timely fashion? Is he or she competent? Answering these questions usually takes much more time, more thinking, more investigation, and more experience.

WARMTH AND COMPETENCE ARE ESSENTIAL
■

Here is what the researchers concluded: If you are a warm and trusting person, the kind of person whom people like, enjoy, and want to be around, you will have lots of friends and good relationships. But if you get the reputation for not being particularly good at your work or, even worse, for being incompetent and undependable, people may still like you, but they will also actually pity you.

The reason is that people instinctively recognize that a nice person who is not very good at their work has a limited future. He will not be successful over the long term. Instead of being a winner, he will be a nonwinner, a person who will not achieve very much in life.

Perhaps the most important ability in the world of work is "depend-ability." This means that people can absolutely depend on you to do an excellent job—on time, every time.

People who participate in karaoke have an expression: Showing up. The question they ask about a performer is, "How is he or she showing up?" This is a description of the totality of the performance of the karaoke singer.

In life, we are always being judged and evaluated by other people, just as we are always judging and evaluating others. Every day, in every situation, you show up in a particular way, and both make and leave a particular impression. The totality of the impressions you make constitutes your personal brand. The question is, How are you showing up?

Your goal is to show up as a top performer. You want people to think about you and talk about you as an excellent person, as someone who really makes a valuable contribution, consistently, in every situation. This is the best reputation or brand you can have.

And everyone knows the truth. Everyone knows who are the best and most productive people in every work environment. So the question for you is, How are you showing up?

THE GREAT PANDEMIC

■

A pandemic is an illness or malady that is spread over a large area and affects an enormous number of people. Today there is a pandemic of poor performance sweeping across the Western world. It is undermining productivity, weakening character, destroying hopes and dreams for the future, cutting off people's desires for achievement and advancement, and keeping millions of people, especially young people, working at lower incomes than they are truly capable of earning.

This pandemic can be called "the curse of electronic interruptions." According to Robert Half International, fully 50 percent of each workday is wasted in activities that contribute no value whatever to the company and that have nothing at all to do with the work at hand. Much of this wasted time is caused by the inability of people to start and work productively all day long.

Most people in their twenties and thirties came into the workplace in the age of the Internet. Today we have Facebook, YouTube, Google, LinkedIn, and Twitter, and smartphones with more than 1,200,000 apps as of 2016. Most of these apps are different forms of entertainment, fun, enjoyment, and time wastage. It is estimated that the average adult today spends three and a half hours each day checking apps, e-mail, and text messages.

Without them even knowing what is happening, people addicted to these distractions will find their hopes and dreams for the future slowly ebbing away. As they spend more time reacting to electronic interruptions, they do less work, and they do it poorly because they are continually being distracted.

YOUR WORLD OF WORK

How is it that so many people are performing and earning far below their potential? You have to go back to children's first experience with work: their school and schoolwork.

Here is what happens: When you are a child and you go to school for the first time, you are usually afraid and insecure. But you very quickly learn that school is full of other children your same age. And what do you do with children your same age? You play! Soon you look forward to school as a place where you can go and play with your friends.

As you advance through school, year after year, school becomes your primary play place. Of course, you must do a certain amount of schoolwork and maintain a certain level of grades in order to be allowed to continue attending the school, but you think primarily of your friends and your social activities rather than the schoolwork itself.

If you are fortunate enough to go on to university, you continue to play with your friends, but now, without supervision! Most people who go to college spend four or five years in an endless cycle of social activities with other people, doing only enough schoolwork to avoid being expelled.

THE WORLD OF WORK
■

When you finish school, you take your first job. You go in to work on the first day a bit nervous and unsure about what is going to happen. Then you are introduced to your co-workers, many of whom are your same age. This reminds you of school. What do you do with people your same age? You play!

Today, the workplace is the primary play place for American adults. It is estimated that the average employee does not really start work until around 11:00 A.M., and then begins winding down about 3:30 in the afternoon.

The first thing people do when they arrive at work is

to "play with their friends." They spend almost 50 percent of their time chatting with co-workers about subjects that have nothing to do with the job they have been hired for. When they are not talking with their co-workers, they are reading their e-mail, sending and receiving messages, checking Facebook postings, looking at what is for sale and where, and responding to various forms of advertising and spam. Suddenly they look up, and the day is gone.

Because so many people see the workplace as a play place, they often resent it when the boss comes by and asks them to actually do some work. They are so preoccupied with the ceaseless flow of electronic interruptions that they have no time to do work of a serious nature.

THE E-MAIL DISEASE

The average adult checks their e-mail 145 times per day. This is why Julie Morgenstern, a time management expert, wrote a book called *Never Check E-Mail in the Morning*. More and more companies and organizations—even the *Harvard Business Review*—are coming to the same conclusion. Spending too much time on e-mail can sabotage your career and make it almost impossible for you to perform at high levels in your job.

The reason e-mail can be so devastating to your current productivity and your future prospects is that each time you send or receive an e-mail, your body releases a tiny amount of dopamine, a stimulant similar to cocaine. This stimulant gives you a mild sense of pleasure, which causes you unconsciously to want to duplicate this feeling. And since you get this feeling by sending or receiving e-mails, checking SMS messages, making phone calls, or otherwise communicating by smartphone or computer, you start doing this all day long. Soon, you can't stop yourself, like an addict.

According to a story in *USA Today*, when you continually respond to e-mails and messages, your brain becomes more and more fatigued. As a result, you lose about ten IQ points in the course of the day. You actually become *dumber* as the day goes on. By the end of the day, your brain is so tired that you have difficulty making even the simplest of decisions, like what to eat for dinner or what to watch on television.

WORK TIME VERSUS PLAY TIME
∎

The solution to your becoming caught up in the irresistible "attraction of distraction" is to remind yourself continually when you go to work that this is productive time; it is not play time.

When you took your job, you entered into an agreement to produce a certain quality and quantity of work in exchange for a certain quantity of money and benefits. You made a promise, and you have a promise to keep. You made a contract, and you are required to comply with the terms of your contract. When you think of work like this, it can change your whole perspective.

Every minute of every day at work, ask these questions:

1. Why am I on the payroll? What have I been hired to accomplish?
2. Is what I am doing right now the reason that I am on the payroll? Is what I am doing the highest and best use of my time?

If you are not doing the most important things that you have been hired to do, stop whatever you are doing and get back to doing whatever it is that you have been hired to do.

WHEN YOU WORK, WORK
■

Here is the great rule for success at work: Work all the time you work.

When you go to work, say hello to your co-workers and then begin work immediately. Put your head down and go flat-out, like a runner coming off the blocks in a race. If people want to chat with you, smile politely and tell them you would love to talk to them after work. Meanwhile, you have things you have to get done and you are on a tight deadline. Eventually, the time wasters, the people who do not value their time or the time of anyone else, will find you uninteresting and will spend more and more time with other people who have more time to waste.

Here is a simple formula for work time. Don't check your e-mail in the morning. Check your e-mail only twice a day, at perhaps 11:00 and 3:00. In between, turn off your e-mail. Turn off all the sounds, bells, and rings that remind you there are incoming messages. Remember, every time you hear one of those sounds, you get a dopamine jolt, distracting you from your work and decreasing your productivity. Leave them off.

FOCUS AND CONCENTRATION
∎

The second keyword for high productivity is *focus*. Your ability to focus single-mindedly on your most important task can do more to help you move ahead rapidly in your career than perhaps any other factor. Electronic interruptions break your focus and distract you from your work, the results you need to get to be successful.

Many people have been seduced by the myth of *multitasking*. They think that they can work on several jobs at a time. But the experts have found that multitasking is really just "task shifting," going back and forth among various tasks, seldom focusing on any one for very long. Even worse, you require about seventeen minutes to refocus on an important task after being distracted, for any reason.

The third keyword for improving productivity is *concentration*. All important work requires single-minded concentration for a sustained period of time until the work is done. This is often called *concentrated mind activity* (CMA). Fortunately, concentration is a skill, or a habit, that you can learn with practice and repetition until it becomes easy and automatic.

THE BIG PAYOFFS
∎

There are two big payoffs for practicing clarity, focus, and concentration all day long at work. The first payoff is that you will become one of the most productive and respected people in your organization. You will get much more done, sooner and of higher quality. More and more important assignments will be given to you. You will gain the attention and respect of your superiors. You will be paid more and promoted faster. Doors of opportunity will open up for you, and sometimes far more rapidly than you can now imagine.

The second big payoff for practicing clarity, focus, and concentration is the way you feel about yourself. All of your work life, and most of your personal life, revolves around the starting and completing of tasks. Each time you start and complete a task, of any size, you get a burst of energy, enthusiasm, and self-esteem. You feel better about yourself. You feel happier. Your brain releases endorphins, nature's "happy drug," and you feel more creative, more calm, more confident, and more personable toward others.

FEEL LIKE A WINNER
■

Here is the formula: Start each day with a list of tasks that you need to complete. Organize the tasks from the most important to the least important. Start work on your most important task, and discipline yourself to work on it nonstop until it is complete.

Whenever you complete any task, you get a jolt of endorphins, which makes you happier and boosts your feelings of self-esteem and personal pride. When you complete a high-value task, you get an even greater feeling of happiness and self-esteem. And when you complete your most important task, like finishing a major assignment at work, you experience a burst of exhilaration that causes you to feel wonderful about yourself. When you develop the habit of starting and completing your most important tasks, you put your entire life and career onto the fast track.

The opposite of this feeling of happiness and personal pride, which comes only from task completion, is the feeling of frustration and dissatisfaction that comes from working hour after hour and feeling that you are accomplishing very little. Remember, results are everything. You will be happy only when you know that you are getting the most important results that are expected of you.

MAKING WORK TIME MORE PRODUCTIVE

∎

There are a series of ways for you to use productive time that will dramatically increase your productivity, performance, output, rewards, and income. Because 95 percent of what you do is determined by your habits, and you learn new habits by practice and repetition, within a month of practicing the following proven techniques, you will double and triple your productivity. You will put yourself on the side of the angels.

MAKE A LIST

The first time management technique is simply to write out a list of everything you have to do before you begin work each day. Even better, make a list of everything you have to do on the following day as the last thing you do when you finish your workday.

When you create a list of everything you have to do the next day, your subconscious mind will then work on that list all night long while you sleep. Often you will wake up in the morning with ideas and insights on how to do the job better and in less time.

If something new comes up, write it down on the list. Refuse to do anything, even making a phone call or sending an e-mail, until you write it down. When you write things down on a list, you can see clearly what is more important and what is less important.

According to Alan Lakein, a time management expert, you will save 25 percent of your time the very first day you begin working from a list and stick with that list. In a matter of three or four weeks, you will develop the habit of making lists for your day and for every project or every multitask activity you have to do. Your productivity will increase immediately.

SET CLEAR PRIORITIES

Prioritize your list before you begin work. Take the time to stand back and think about what you have to do, recognizing that you will never be able to get everything done. No matter how productive you are, there will always be too many tasks for you to complete. You're always going to have to choose which tasks to do first, which tasks to do second, and which tasks to do not at all.

Apply the 80/20 Rule to your list. As you recall, this rule says that 20 percent of your activities will account for 80 percent of your results. If you have a list of ten activities planned for a particular day, two of those activities will be worth more than the other eight put together. Sometimes, of course, there will be a single task that is more important than all the others put together.

Remember, it is not the amount of time that you put in, it is the value of the work and the things you achieve in that time. Your job is to focus on accomplishments rather than activities. Allocate your time based on the value of the task, and do the most important first.

THE ABCDE METHOD
■

Practice the *ABCDE Method*. Before you start your workday, go through your list and write one of these five letters before each task or activity. Think about the likely *consequences* of completing or not completing each task. Something is important to a degree to which it has big potential consequences. Something is unimportant to the degree to which it has low or no potential consequences. Consequences are everything.

Successful, highly productive people, spend most of their time working on activities that have big potential consequences. Unsuccessful people often work harder and longer hours, but they spend too much of their time working on activities that have few or no consequences at all. It doesn't really matter if they complete them or not.

Put the letters A, B, C, D, or E next to each task on your list. An A activity is something that you *must do*. It has serious potential consequence for completion or noncompletion. If you don't do this task or get it done on time, there are going to be serious problems. These are the most important things that you do each day.

Put a B in front of activities that you *should do*, activities that have mild potential consequences if they are done or not done. You need to get to these tasks sooner or later, but they are not as important as your A tasks. The rule is that you never do a B task when there is an A task left undone.

A C task is something that would be *nice to do*, but it has no consequences at all, one way or the other. Checking your e-mail, phoning home, having coffee with a co-worker, are all activities that are nice to do but it does not matter at all whether you do them or not.

SELECT YOUR TASKS

Unfortunately, the great majority of people spend most of their time doing B and C tasks, and they think that because they are doing them at their workplace they are actually working. But this is not true. Just because you are at work does not mean that you are indeed working.

Put a D next to all tasks you can delegate to anyone else who can do them who receives a lower income or hourly rate than you do. If you aspire to earn $25 per hour ($50,000 per year) or $50 an hour ($100,000 per year), do not spend your time doing tasks that someone else can do for $10 an hour.

An E task is something that you can eliminate and it won't make any difference at all. It may be a task that you have been doing for a while, but it is no longer important. It may no longer be your task to do. It can be eliminated safely and have no consequences at all for your career.

ORGANIZE YOUR LIST

Now, go back over your list and organize your A tasks by priority by writing A-1, A-2, A-3, and so on next to your most important tasks. Do the same for your B tasks. Finally, start on your A-1 task, your most important and valuable use of your time. Resolve to concentrate single-mindedly on that one task until it is 100 percent complete. Persevere without diversion or distraction.

This simple formula—making a list, prioritizing it, and then starting and completing your most important task—is the formula for doubling and tripling the quality and quantity of your output at work. It is the key to high results. And remember, results are everything.

INCREASE YOUR ROE

Business strategy is focused on helping the company increase its return on equity (ROE), its return on capital invested. This means that the company wants to get the very highest sales and profit possible from its money and efforts.

Your *personal* capital is your physical, mental, and emotional energy. Your goal is to earn the very most you can from your work, to increase your personal ROE as well—your return on energy.

Every minute that you spend planning your work will save you at least 10 minutes in getting your work done. It takes only 10 to 12 minutes for you to plan your entire day. But you will get back two hours of productive time, 120 minutes, just by planning your work before you begin. That is more than a 1,000 percent return on energy.

Time and money are interchangeable. They can be either spent or invested. If you spend time or money, they are gone forever. You can never get them back. But if you *invest* time and money, you can earn a return that may go on for years. When you invest your money in an asset that yields a return, you can earn money year after year. This process of investing is the foundation of most fortunes.

When you invest your time and money back into yourself, becoming better and better at what you do, that investment can give you an increase in income, a higher return on energy, for many years. If you then reinvest your higher income back into yourself, you will soon be one of the most valuable and highest-paid people in your business.

THE LAW OF THREE

Practice the *Law of Three* in your work. This law says that no matter how many tasks you have to complete in your work, only three of those tasks will account for 90 percent of the value of your contribution to your company and to yourself.

When working with my clients, I ask them to make a list of everything they did in the course of a week or a month. They come back to me with twenty or thirty, sometimes even fifty, tasks that they felt were part of their job description.

Then I would explain to them that there are only three things they do in the course of their workday that account for 90 percent of the value of everything they do. This means that everything you do that is *not* one of those three main tasks falls into the bottom 10 percent in terms of value.

The key to increasing your productivity is for you to identify your three most important tasks and then work on them exclusively, while ignoring all the rest.

Start by making a list of everything you do.

To identify your three most important tasks, take a look at your list and then ask the *three magic questions*:

1. If I could only do one task on this list, all day long, which one activity would contribute the greatest value to my work and to my company?

   Whatever your answer is to that question, put a circle around it.

2. If I could only do two things on this list, all day long, what would be the second activity that would enable me to contribute the greatest value to my business or my work?

   The answer to this question is not as easy as the first, but it's usually quite clear.

3. If I could only do three things on this list, all day long, what would be the third activity

that would enable me to contribute the most value?

When you ask yourself these questions and become clear about the answers, you will be astonished to see how true this formula is. If you just did those three things all day long, you would probably transform your career.

There are four corollaries of the Law of Three:

1. *Do fewer things.* You will never get caught up. You will never be able to do everything on your list. To get control of your life you must stop doing an enormous number of small things.

2. *Do more important things.* Do the top three tasks that you have identified, and nothing else, until you have no more of those major tasks to do.

3. *Do your most important tasks more of the time, preferably all day long.* The more time you spend doing the most important things, the more productive you will be on the outside and the happier you will feel on the inside.

4. *Get better at your most important tasks.* Continual self-improvement in the area of your most important tasks is the best investment that you can make. It enables you to dramatically increase your productivity, performance, and output and to get more done in a shorter period of time.

Resolve today that you are going to earn the reputation as the hardest working person in your organization. But don't tell anybody. Keep it to yourself.

Imagine that there is a contest for the most productive person in your business, but you are the only person who knows about the contest. Instead of telling anybody, let people reach their own conclusions by watching you at work. And remember: *Work all the time you work.*

<<< ACTION EXERCISES >>>

1. Make a list every day of everything that you plan to do that day.

2. Set priorities on your list and start work on the one activity that represents the most valuable use of your time.

3. Discipline yourself to start on your most important task and to work single-mindedly on that one task until it is complete.

3

INCOME
IMPROVEMENT TIME

Thought is the original source of all

wealth, all success, all material

gain, all great discoveries and

inventions, and of all achievement.

—CLAUDE M. BRISTOL

Everyone wants to earn more money, to be highly paid, and to achieve financial independence in his or her career. The way you think about your income, and how you can increase it, is one of the most important mental skills you can develop.

Sometimes, I open a seminar by asking, "What is your most valuable *financial* asset?"

The audience usually thinks about this question for a while and then throws out some answers such as "my house," "my bank account," and "my business."

Then I explain that your most valuable financial asset is your *earning ability*. This is defined as your ability to get results that people will pay you for. You could lose all your money through no fault of your own, but as long as you are left with your earning ability, you could go back into the marketplace and earn it all back again. This is what many successful people do throughout their lifetimes.

Your earning ability is the total accumulation of all your knowledge, skills, experience, study, hard work, and results you have acquired over the course of your life and your career. It has taken you your whole life to develop.

APPRECIATING OR DEPRECIATING?

Because your earning ability is an asset, like any other asset, it can be either *appreciating* or *depreciating* in value over time. It can be appreciating when you are continually upgrading your knowledge and skills, making yourself become more and more valuable, doing more of those tasks that people value highly and are willing to pay you for.

Your earning ability can be a "depreciating asset" if you are not continually upgrading your skills and abilities through study and hard work on yourself. But because of rapid change in our economy, and the continual demand for new skills, your earning ability never stays at the same level.

Gary Becker, the Nobel Prize–winning economist at the University of Chicago, noted that we do not have an "income gap" in our society. Instead, we have a "skills gap." People who have skills that are in high demand, skills that enable employers to get excellent results that they can turn into money by producing and selling more of their products and services, are always in demand, always employed, and always paid well.

SKILLS BECOME OBSOLETE
■

On the other hand, those people who have obsolete skills, skills that are no longer in demand, often remain unemployed for many months, and even years. What Becker found was that the primary difference between employed people in the top 20 percent, those whose incomes were increasing an average of 11 percent per year, and the people in the bottom 80 percent, those whose incomes were increasing at 3 percent or less per year, was their commitment to continuous learning. The highest-paid people were always reading, learning, and upgrading their skills.

Anders Ericsson, the founder of elite performance studies, concluded that most people work for the first year to learn their jobs well enough so as not to get fired. After that, they never get any better. They never improve. Ten years after they started their job, they're no more productive than they were after one year. This seems to apply to 80 percent of people working today.

LIFELONG LEARNERS
∎

The people in the top 20 percent are lifelong learners. They are continually adding to their repertoire of knowledge and skills. They read, study, and practice new ideas. They never let up the pressure on themselves to improve and grow.

As a Fortune 500 CEO recently said, "Our only real source of sustainable competitive advantage is our ability to learn and apply new ideas faster than our competition."

These words apply to you. Your only personal source of sustainable competitive advantage, of keeping yourself at a high level of employability and income, is your ability to learn and practice new skills that people need to get more and better results.

Ericsson found that high performers in every field spend much more time practicing and upgrading their skills than low performers. This difference accounted for most of the large income disparities we see in our society.

IDENTIFY YOUR MOST IMPORTANT SKILL
∎

Ericsson investigated executives who started work with large companies and who, over the years, moved into high positions of management, sometimes becoming the CEO or president, where they earned as much as 301 times (2016) the average income of the people who worked in their companies.

He found that most of these people practiced a simple strategy they had used throughout their careers. As soon as they started at their first job, they went to their boss and asked him, "What one skill, if I was really good at it, would help me to make a more valuable contribution at my job?"

The boss would tell the employee that if he was really good at marketing, or team building, or making presentations, or reading financial statements, or something else, he would be able to do his job much better and make a more valuable contribution.

The new employee would take that advice, like a dog catching a stick and running with it, and begin work immediately to develop that skill. He would set the development of this skill as a goal and create a learning plan. He would make a list of all the things that he could do to become better in that area. He would find out the books that he should read, the courses and workshops he should attend, and the audio programs he could listen to on the way to work.

THE MAGIC NUMBER
■

Here is the magic number. Ericsson found that these top people invested two hours per day, five days per week, to learn new skills.

There are 168 hours in each week (twenty-four hours times seven days). By investing ten of those hours, on average, people starting off at the bottom of their corporations, at the beginning of their careers, were able to continually move up, faster and faster. As they developed more knowledge and skills, they continued to increase their earning ability, their ability to get results.

While their friends were out socializing, partying, and watching sports on television, these high-achievers were carving out two hours each day, five days each week, to get better and better at their work.

Albert Einstein wrote, "Compounding is the most powerful force in the universe." This applies to money and to skills as well.

What these successful executives discovered at an early stage of their careers was that each time they learned a new skill, they could combine that skill with other skills, compounding the total value of all their knowledge and skills. Thus these employees became more and more valuable.

Over the years, I have found that many people are only one skill away from doubling their income. If they could develop one more key skill, leveraged times the skills and experience they already had, they could be twice as valuable to their company, and be paid twice as much.

SEE YOURSELF AS SELF-EMPLOYED
■

The top 3 percent of people in every industry accept high levels of responsibility for themselves, for everything they do, and for everything they become. As a result, they view themselves as self-employed. They act as if they owned the company they work in.

Robert Reich, a former U.S. secretary of labor, said that when he went into a company, he could immediately determine the type of culture the company had developed. He said it was contained in the pronouns the employees used when they talked about the company and themselves.

In the top companies, people would use the words *we* and *us* and *our*. In the top companies, people felt and acted as if the company belonged to them. They were fully engaged. They accepted high levels of responsibility for the company's results.

In the lower-performing companies, people use the pronouns *they, them,* and *their.* They viewed the company as something completely apart from themselves, an entity that provided them with a job and a paycheck, and that was all. This is why it is estimated that fully 65 percent of employees today are officially disengaged from their work. They are going through the motions each day, putting in minimum effort, reading the want ads on the Internet, and dreaming about doing different work.

YOU ARE THE PRESIDENT

But not the top people. The top people realize that they are the chief executive officers, the presidents, of their own careers. They see themselves as the presidents of a company called "You, Inc."

Earl Nightingale once said, "The worst mistake you can ever make is to think that you work for anyone else but yourself." You are always self-employed.

No matter who signs your paycheck, you are always on your own payroll. You are always working for yourself. You are the president of a personal services corporation with one employee, yourself. You have only one product to sell in a competitive market—your own personal services.

Your rewards in life and in your career will be determined by the value of your services to others, by your ability to contribute to your company, and by your ability to add value continuously throughout your career.

WHAT DETERMINES YOUR INCOME?
■

Your income will be largely determined by three factors: The work you do, how well you do it, and the difficulty of replacing you.

If you are not happy with the amount you are being paid, you must do different work or you must do your current work better, and you must become indispensable to your company so they would have tremendous difficulty finding someone to replace you.

Because of these three factors, unemployment or underemployment, high or low income, and earning less than your true potential are largely *self-determined*, personal choices. Over time, each person largely decides his or her own income. Each person decides how much he or she is going to earn. Each person decides their own financial future by the things they do and by the things that they fail to do.

Ludwig von Mises, the great economist, wrote, "Every action has a consequence or consequences." Your ability to accurately predict the consequences of your actions is a mark of the superior thinker. Von Mises then pointed out that *anything* that has a consequence can be considered an action, even an inaction, even doing nothing in certain circumstances.

Just as there are things that you do that have consequences or results in your life, the things that you *don't* do can have consequences as well. And sometimes your *inactions* have greater consequences than you can imagine.

A person who comes to work at the last minute, spends most of their day socializing with their friends, takes long coffee breaks and lunch hours, and leaves at the earliest possible minute is engaging in actions that will soon have negative consequences for his career. Failing to upgrade your skills, to use your time well, or to work hard at your most important tasks are *inactions* that can have enormous negative consequences as well.

NATURE IS NEUTRAL
■

Everyone wants to earn more money, to be paid more, to be promoted faster, and to achieve financial independence. But Nature is neutral. She plays no favorites. She is like the statue of justice wearing a blindfold. Nature simply says, "If you want to take more out, you must put more in."

Nature also says, "You cannot take more out than you put in."

One of my favorite quotes is from Goethe, the German philosopher. He wrote, "Nature understands no jesting. She is always true. Always severe. She is always right and the errors and faults are always those of man. The man incapable of appreciating her, she despises and only to the apt, the pure, and the true does she resign herself and reveal her secrets."

These words are applicable to the world of work, in every respect.

Nature says that you can have all the money you want, but you'll have to earn it by serving other people with the things they want and need and are willing to pay for it.

Ely Callaway, founder of Callaway Golf, once said, "Your business is designed today to get you exactly the results you are getting today—and it could be no other way."

It is the same with you and your personal services corporation. Your life and career, including your skill set, what you do, and how well you do it are giving you exactly the results you are getting today. If you want to get more and better results, you must do your work better, increase your value, and, especially, develop new and better skills that enable you to make an even greater contribution to your company.

THINK ABOUT THE CONSEQUENCES
■

Your ability to learn and apply new knowledge and skill has some of the biggest potential consequences of all for your life. This means that if you continually learn and grow, or fail to learn and grow, the consequences in your life can be enormous.

The acquisition or development of one key skill in addition to your existing skill set can often double your value and your income quite quickly.

Some of the most important words in business today are *business model* and *value proposition*. In both cases, they ask these questions of a product:

What is it?

What does it do?

What problems does it solve?

What results does it get?

These questions apply to you and your personal services as well. They apply to the rapidly changing needs, desires, and demands of customers (employers) in response to competition and market forces.

These are questions that you must take the time to ask and answer again and again throughout your career. This time spent in self-assessment can be some of the most important and valuable time of your life.

What are your core skills, your core competencies?

What is the most important and valuable work that you do?

What are the most important results and benefits you achieve for your employer and your business?

What are you good at today? What will you need to be good at six months or a year from now to be successful in your career?

> What one skill, if you were absolutely excel-
> lent at it, would have the greatest positive
> impact on your life and career?
> What one skill would help you the most to
> double your income?

The last question is perhaps the most important go-
forward question of your career. As the speed of growth
in information, technology, and competition acceler-
ates, your answer to this question will change. What is
your plan to develop this skill?

DEVELOP A PLAN FOR PERSONAL EXCELLENCE
∎

What is your plan to become one of the top people in
your field?

People don't plan to fail; they just fail to plan. Your
goal should be to learn one skill at a time, one after
another. The interesting discovery is that as you concentrate single-mindedly on the learning and development of your most important skill, you start to improve,
almost unconsciously, in every other important skill as
well.

By focusing on individual skill development, you
change the way you think and the way you use your

time, hour by hour and day by day. You become a learning machine, constantly absorbing new knowledge.

Top people dedicate themselves to continuous learning, as if their entire future career depended on it, because it does.

Resolve today to include a learning time into your life, every day, every week, every month. Create a learning space in your home or apartment. Set a schedule to study for a certain period of time each day, and discipline yourself to stick to your schedule.

Be willing to pay the price of success, in advance, over and over, for years if necessary, to get to the top of your field.

The good news is that you can learn anything you need to learn to achieve any goal that you can set for yourself. And the more you learn, the more you can learn.

When you concentrate on learning new subjects, you activate more and more of your brainpower, your ganglia and neurons, which are connected to hundreds and thousands of other neurons. As a result, you get smarter and smarter. Your mind functions faster and with greater clarity. You can then learn even more new subjects faster and faster.

When you become a lifelong learner, your potential has no limit.

<<< ACTION EXERCISES >>>

1. Identify the one skill that, if you were excellent at it, would enable you to make a more valuable contribution than any other skill.
2. Set it as a goal to develop this skill, create a learning plan to attain this skill, and then work single-mindedly to master this one skill, no matter how long it takes.
3. Set aside a minimum of ten hours per week during which you learn, study, and develop your most important skill.

4

SPARE TIME

All riches have their origin in
mind. Wealth is in ideas—
not money.

—ROBERT COLLIER

One of the most important times of your life is a time period that few people think of: your spare time.

There are 168 hours in a week. The average person works 8 hours per day (40 hours a week); sleeps 8 hours per day (56 hours a week); and dresses, eats, and travels to work 4 hours per day (28 hours a week). These tasks use up 124 hours, leaving 44 hours a week as spare time.

Unfortunately, the average person spends most of this time socializing, watching television or in entertainment activities of some kind, such as social media, television, conversations with friends, and other leisure time activities.

But what you do with your spare time can make all the difference between success and failure in life. You can spend it on pleasurable activities or you can invest it in your future.

THE BY-PRODUCTS OF LIFE
∎

Many manufacturers, especially those using large quantities of raw materials and natural resources in the production process, throw off large quantities of by-products. Surrounding many factories you will see large slag heaps of by-products that eventually must be disposed of in some way.

Over the years, with advances in science, these by-products are often turned into new products to be sold. Many by-products that were once thrown away can now be converted into useful products, thereby using up more and more of the by-product, leaving less and less to be disposed of.

Sometimes, the by-product of a manufacturing process turns out to be more profitable than the main product being produced.

For decades, the Bayer Chemical Corporation of Germany created large quantities of acetylsalicylic acid in the process of manufacturing other chemical products. This acid, in crystal powder, was piled in large heaps outside the factory before being hauled away for disposal.

Over a period of months, a Bayer executive looking out his window noticed that many of the workers arriving on Monday morning were stopping to scoop up and gulp down a handful of this crystalline powder.

When the workers were asked the reason for this, they replied that this powder was a great painkiller that took away headaches and muscular pains they got from overworking and overdrinking on the weekends.

This led to the discovery of the remarkable properties of what Bayer trademarked as Aspirin.

Today Bayer aspirin is one of the most popular and profitable all-purpose, over-the-counter remedies in the world. Bayer aspirin has made a fortune for the company, many billions of dollars, and perhaps more than it was earning from the original chemical of which the aspirin was a by-product.

YOUR PERSONAL BY-PRODUCT

■

In your life, your spare time is a by-product as well. By using this spare time intelligently, rather than wasting it or discarding it, you can become more valuable, be paid more money, and even become one of the top people in your field.

Spare time is the real by-product of your busy life.

If you are living a normal life, you have about four hours per day of discretionary time, and perhaps sixteen spare hours on the weekend.

How you spend this spare time largely determines

your future and much of what you achieve in the months and years ahead.

When you continually invest your by-product, your spare time, by learning new ideas and developing new skills, by some mysterious process, this additional knowledge and skills combines with your existing skill base, allowing you to multiply your results and eventually earn much more than the other people around you.

BECOME A HIGH EARNER
▪

The 80/20 Rule says that the top 20 percent of earners in any field earn 80 percent of the money paid out in that field. You have heard this before, but have you ever worked out on paper what this actually means?

Imagine that there are 100 employees in a company that has a total payroll per month of $1 million. But the top 20 percent of those employees, twenty people, will earn 80 percent of the total amount, or $800,000. The other eighty people, 80 percent, will earn $200,000.

When you continue with this calculation, you find that the average income of the top 20 percent is $40,000 per person ($800,000 divided by 20).

The average income of the bottom 80 percent will be $2,500 each ($200,000 divided by 80).

What is the ratio of income between the high earners and the low earners? It is $40,000 divided by $2,500, or a difference of sixteen times in income in exchange for working the same eight hours.

All over the world, this principle holds true. The people in the top 20 percent earn on average sixteen times the average pay of the bottom 80 percent. The people in the top 20 percent of the top 20 percent (the top 4 percent) earn much, much more.

MY OWN STORY
■

When I was twenty-four years old, with holes in my shoes, and struggling to get started in direct commission sales, another salesman asked me if I had ever heard about the 80/20 Rule—that the top 20 percent in sales earn 80 percent of the income.

I had never heard that statistic, the Pareto Principle, before. But at that moment, it suddenly occurred to me that I had a choice. I could earn a little or I could earn a lot. At that time I was earning a little, very little. So I made a decision that I was going to do whatever it took to get into the top 20 percent.

That decision changed my life. From that day onward, I began asking successful people what they were doing differently from the way I did things. I read books written by successful people. I listened to audio programs on success and sales recorded by successful people. I attended seminars given by successful people in which they explained exactly what they had done to start at the bottom and get to the top.

One thing I learned was that everyone in the top 20 percent started in the bottom 20 percent. Everyone who is doing well today was once doing poorly. Almost all rich people today were once poor. And the major turning point in the lives of the top people was when they made the decision to become one of the best people in their field.

Resolve today to become a member of the 20 percent in your field. If you are already in the top 20 percent, decide to be in the top 10 percent.

SET A CLEAR GOAL FOR YOURSELF
∎

You can't hit a target that you can't see. You can't achieve a goal if you don't know what it is. Whatever field you are in today, find out how much the top 20 percent are earning. Then set their income level as your initial goal.

Here is the good news: Once you have decided to get

into the top 20 percent in your field, nothing and no one can stop you—as long as you don't quit. Your own determination is stronger than any other influence.

Make a decision! I have never met anyone, anywhere in the world (120 countries) who failed to get into the top 20 percent after they made that do-or-die decision to do whatever was necessary to achieve it.

And I never met anyone who got into the top 20 percent until they made that decision and then backed it up with months and even years of hard, hard work.

The motto of the top person is: "I will, until!"

The problem in society today is not an income gap. Instead, it is a skills gap. The highest paid people have skills that are in demand. The lowest paid workers do not.

But skills are not handed out like Halloween treats. They are developed over long time periods of patient, determined effort.

CONTINUE TO LEARN AND GROW
∎

People in the top 20 percent use their spare time well. They continue to learn and grow throughout their careers. As a result, their incomes increase at an average of 11 percent per year. At 11 percent per year, with the power of compounding, your income will double every 6.7 years.

This means that, if you start off at the age of twenty getting better and better each year, studying an average of ten hours per week, by the age of twenty-seven, you will be earning twice as much as you were when you started. By the age of thirty-four, you will double your income again and be earning four times as much. You will be one of the highest paid people in your field.

If you keep improving, increasing your productivity, performance, and income by 11 percent per year, by age thirty-nine you will double your income again and be on your way to personal wealth. If you keep this up throughout your life, by the time you reach your forties and fifties, you will be in the top 10 percent, or even in the top 1 percent, of money earners in the world today.

People in the top 20 percent continue to learn and grow throughout their careers. People in the bottom 80 percent stop learning and developing new skills as soon as they master the basic requirements of their jobs. Which one are you? Which one do you want to be in the years ahead? Resolve today to use ten hours of your spare time each week to invest in your future. It will be one of the best decisions you ever make.

<<< ACTION EXERCISES >>>

1. Put the power of compounding to work in your life by acquiring additional skills in your spare time.

2. Resolve to join the top 20 percent of income earners in your field.

3. Find out what the highest earners do in their spare time to stay ahead and then do the same things over and over until they become habits of thought and action.

5

WORK TIME

Be true to the best you know. This
is your high ideal. If you do your
best, you cannot do more.

—H. W. DRESSER

The way you use work time will determine your success, advancement, and income as much, if not more, than any other factor. The tragedy is that most people do not work anywhere near their true capacity.

There is nothing that will move you ahead faster than for you to get a reputation for good work habits. When you are highly productive at work, you will attract more and more opportunities. But one of the biggest obstacles to high performance is the structure of the work itself.

There is a saying: "You can't get any work done at work."

The reason is so much of your time is taken up by other people and situations, especially working with other people and groups, both within your business and on the outside. Much of your time is taken up responding to the demands of others.

Nonetheless, it is essential that you learn to work with and around groups of other people, each of whom has complementary strengths, knowledge, and abilities and whose help and participation you need to do your job. The question, however, is always, How do you get your work done at work?

BRILLIANT ON THE BASICS

■

Let's do a quick review of the basics of using your time well:

1. Set clear goals and objectives. You must know exactly why you are working and what you want to accomplish.
2. Plan out your work in detail, on paper. You need detailed plans of action, organized by sequence and priority for productive work.
3. Set clear priorities on your tasks. You must always work on your highest value activities.
4. Work all the time you work. You must learn how to concentrate single-mindedly on one thing, the most important thing, at any given time, and stay at it until it is complete. This takes tremendous willpower and self-discipline, but the payoff in career success makes the effort truly worth it.

Time is the one indispensable ingredient of accomplishment. Everything you want to do at work requires time. The only way you can get enough time to do the things that can really make a difference in your work and your life is by conserving time that you would normally spend doing something else.

You are surrounded by people and situations that waste your time and undermine your effectiveness all day long. Only by practicing rigorous self-discipline can you free yourself from these thieves of time.

THE SEVEN MAJOR TIME WASTERS
■

There are seven major time wasters in the world of work, which have been identified from hundreds of studies and opinion surveys. Your ability to deal with them effectively will largely determine how successful you will be in your career.

I. Telephone, E-mail, and Text Interruptions

The first major time waster is interruption by telephone, e-mail, and SMS. When the telephone rings or the e-mail dings, your train of thought is broken and you're distracted from the task at hand. When you hang up the phone or turn away from the screen, you find it hard to get back to the work in front of you.

There are seven ways to deal with telephone and e-mail interruptions:

1. Use the telephone and e-mail as business tools. Get on and off the telephone or computer fast. Don't socialize when you are working. Make your calls or messages as efficient as possible. You must discipline yourself to use the telephone and the computer as business tools during the hours from nine to five. This applies to your smartphone as well.

2. Have your e-mails and calls screened or screen them yourself. Find out who is on the phone before you answer. Overcome the natural curiosity that wells up in you when people who you don't know call you. Find out why they are calling before you take the phone call.

3. Whenever possible, set aside periods of the day when you allow no interruptions. Don't become a slave to a ringing phone, a binging e-mail, or a beeping text message. Leave things off. There is nothing so important that you cannot get back to it later when it is more convenient for you.

4. When you make a call or send an e-mail message, set clear callback or response times. Tell others the time that you will be available to respond to the message or phone call. Avoid playing telephone or e-mail tag. Leave a telephone number if it is an emergency.

5. Batch your calls and your e-mail activities. Use the learning curve. Make all of your telephone calls or e-mail responses at once. Don't spread them throughout the day. Sometimes you can accumulate your phone calls or e-mail messages up to 11:00 A.M. and then return them all by noon. Then you can accumulate them again up to 3:30 P.M. and return them all by 4:30.

6. Plan your calls and e-mail in advance. Think about a business call as a meeting and write out an outline or agenda for the items you want to cover in the call or typed message.

7. Take good notes. When talking on the phone, write down every key point made by the other person and you. Never answer a telephone without a pad of paper in front of you and a pen in your hand. The *power* is always on the side of the person with the best notes.

2. Unexpected Visitors

The second major time waster is unexpected visitors. Drop-in visitors can be extremely time-consuming. These are people from within your company or from the outside. They drop by your office, disrupt your work, break your train of thought, and impair your effectiveness. Sometimes they talk endlessly about unimportant matters and keep you from your work.

You must find ways to avoid this time waster at all costs. Here are five things you can do:

1. Create a quiet time for work. Specify a time during the day when you will concentrate on your work. During this time, allow no interruptions. Turn everything off. Get yourself a Do Not Disturb sign and put it on your door. Make it clear that when that sign is out, you do not want to be disturbed for any reason by anyone except in an emergency.

2. Stand up quickly when unwelcome visitors walk into your office or come to your workplace, as though you were just leaving. Start moving as though you were on your way out. Tell the time waster that you are really swamped today and you have a lot that you

have to get done. When someone interrupts you by phone, tell them that you were just leaving, and you are in a bit of a hurry. This will prompt them to get straight to the point.

3. Bring the discussion to a close. When the meeting has gone on long enough, you can say, "There's one more thing before you go." Finish off the conversation with anything you can think of, shake hands, and then go back to work.

4. Arrange specific meeting times. To deal effectively with drop-in visitors, you can arrange specific times to meet that are convenient for both of you. Make appointments to get together with the people in your office. Make appointments with your staff and let them know that, at certain times of the day, your door is open and you will be available.

5. Avoid wasting the time of others. Make every effort to avoid being a drop-in visitor yourself. If you do drop in on someone else without warning, always be polite enough to ask, "Is this a good time to talk or can we get together later?" Ask for their permission in advance. It is amazing how many people unconsciously waste the time of others and don't even know it.

If you want to increase your efficiency, ask others, "What do I do that wastes your time?" Be prepared for an earful. And whatever the other person says, refuse to defend or explain. Just thank her, and listen without interrupting.

3. Meetings

The third time waster is meetings, both planned and unplanned. They consume 40 to 50 percent of your time. They can be planned and organized, involving several people, or they can be one-on-one in an office or in the hallway. Whenever you meet to talk with one or more people, you are having a meeting. Because of poor planning and preparation, many meetings are unnecessary or largely a waste of time.

However, meetings are not an evil. Meetings are a necessary business tool for exchanging information, solving problems, and reviewing progress. But they must be managed and they must be used effectively.

Before scheduling a meeting, determine its cost. Remember, each meeting costs the hourly rate of the people attending, multiplied by the number of hours spent in the meeting. Meetings should, therefore, be treated as an actual dollar expenditure with an expected value or rate of return on the investment.

Here are seven ways that you can make meetings more efficient:

1. Ask whether the meeting is necessary. If it is not necessary, avoid holding it whenever possible. If it is not necessary for an individual to attend a particular meeting, make sure that he knows he does not have to be there.

2. Create an agenda. If you have determined that the meeting is necessary, establish a clear purpose and write an agenda or make a list of everything that has to be covered. Next to each item, put the name of the person who is expected to address that particular issue. This also applies to one-on-one meetings with your boss, subordinates, customers, suppliers, and everyone else. You will be amazed at how much faster and more efficiently the meeting will progress when there is a written agenda that everyone is following.

3. Start and stop on time. Set a schedule for the beginning of the meeting, and set a time for the end of the meeting. The worst types of meetings are those that start at a specific time but have no clearly determined ending time. Here is another rule: Don't wait for the late-

comer. Assume the latecomer is not coming at all and start at the designated time. It is unfair to punish the people who are on time by making them wait for the person who gets there late, if at all.

4. Cover the most important items first. When you draw up the agenda, apply the 80/20 Rule. Organize the agenda so that the top 20 percent of items are the first items to be discussed. This way, if you run out of time, you will have covered the items that represent 80 percent of the value of the meeting before the time runs out.

5. Summarize each conclusion. When you discuss an item on your meeting agenda, summarize the discussion and get closure. Get agreement and completion on each item before you go on to the next one. Restate what has been decided on and agreed to for each item before you proceed.

6. Assign specific responsibility. Once you have made a decision, assign responsibility to a specific person for the actions agreed on and set deadlines. Remember, discussion and agreement without an assignment of responsibility

and a deadline for completion is merely a conversation.

7. Keep notes and circulate minutes. A key to getting maximum effectiveness from meetings is to keep accurate notes as you go along and then to circulate the minutes of the meeting within twenty-four hours whenever possible. The person who takes accurate minutes from a meeting and then can access those notes a week or a month later always has greater power and influence than someone working from memory.

4. Fire Fighting

The fourth time waster is fire fighting and emergencies. Just when you get settled down to work on an important project, something totally unexpected happens that takes you away from your main task, for a few minutes or even for hours.

When an emergency or crisis occurs, here are six ways to cope:

1. Think before acting. Remember, action without thinking is the cause of every failure. Take a deep breath, calm down, and remain objective. Refuse to react or overreact. Instead, just stop and think. Take the time to find out what happened. Be clear about the problem before you act.

2. Delegate responsibility. There is a rule that says, "If it is not necessary for you to decide, it is necessary for you *not* to decide." If you can possibly delegate the responsibility for handling the crisis to someone else, by all means do so. Someone else might be much better qualified to deal with the situation than you, or maybe it is someone else's responsibility in the first place.

3. Write it down. Whatever the crisis, write it down before you take action. When you write down a problem it helps keep your mind cool, calm, clear, and objective. Record exactly what has happened before you do anything.

4. Get the facts. Don't assume anything. The facts are perhaps the most important elements of all in a crisis. Ask questions. Find out what occurred, including details about when,

where, and how it happened. Determine who was involved. Then ask, What can we do now? Remember, the facts don't lie. The more facts you gather, the more capable you will be of dealing with the problem when you take action.

5. Develop a policy. If you find yourself dealing with a recurring crisis, one that happens again and again, develop a policy that is simple enough so that ordinary people can implement it. When a crisis occurs for the first or second time, it may require tremendous intelligence, experience, and energy to deal with it effectively. But if a crisis or problem has a tendency to repeat itself, and you cannot find the way to eliminate the crisis in advance, you should by all means develop a system so that the average person can deal with the problem in your absence.

6. Plan for the worst. Problems and crises are normal, natural, and unavoidable in the history of any company or organization. One of the qualities of great leaders throughout history is that they develop the ability to think ahead and determine what could possibly go wrong. They then plan for contingencies in

advance. When something goes wrong, they are ready to move quickly. They have already thought it through. Ask yourself, What are the worst things that could happen in my business or personal life, and how would I handle them?

5. Procrastination

The fifth biggest time waster is procrastination. Procrastination is not only the thief of time. It is the thief of life. Your ability to stop procrastinating and get on with the work can change your life.

Here are seven ways to overcome procrastination:

1. Think on paper. Prepare thoroughly. List every step of the job in advance. Break the job down into its constituent parts before you begin.
2. Gather all the materials and work tools you will need before you begin so you won't have to get up or move until the task is done.
3. Do one small thing to get started. Often the first 20 percent of the task accounts for 80 percent of the value. Once you get started, it is much easier to keep going.

4. "Salami slice" the task. Sometimes the best way to complete a major job or project is to take a small slice and complete just that one piece.

5. Practice the "Swiss cheese" technique. Just as a block of Swiss cheese is full of holes, you treat your task like a block of cheese and you punch holes in it, selecting a five-minute part of the job and doing just that.

6. Start from the outside and complete the smaller tasks first. Often this will help you to overcome procrastination and get you started on the big task.

7. Start from the inside and do the larger tasks first. Discipline yourself to start on the one item that will take the most time and require the most effort. Once you complete this task, all the other tasks will seem easier by comparison.

6. Socializing and Idle Conversations

The sixth time waster is socializing and idle conversation, both one-on-one, and online. Socializing takes up an enormous amount of time. It has been estimated that as much as 75 percent of time at work is spent interacting with other people. Unfortunately, at least half of this time is spent in idle chatter that has nothing to do with work. Socializing takes time away from getting the job done.

Too much socializing can sabotage your career if you become well known for it. Too many people are time wasters and time-consumers. They are working well below their capacity so they have lots of time to socialize and engage in idle chatter. Here are some ideas you can use to avoid getting trapped into excessive socializing.

Socialize at appropriate times. Arrange to do your socializing at coffee breaks, lunch, and after work. Whenever you find yourself being drawn into a nonwork-related conversation with colleagues, say, "Well, I have to get back to work." Break off the conversation politely and then move on. It's amazing how often the use of these words will cause other people to get back to work as well.

Focus on results. You are a knowledge worker. Relationships with other knowledge workers are unavoidably time-consuming. Some of the most valuable time you spend at work is talking through and working out problems and solutions to the challenges facing your business. But these conversations must be focused on results, not on the latest football game or sharing stories about golf or summer holidays. Relationships, communications, and discussion with knowledge workers must be continually focused on the results that you and your work colleagues are trying to accomplish.

7. Indecision and Delay

The seventh major time waster is indecision and delay. Indecision costs more time than most people realize. It can generate unnecessary paperwork, correspondence, and tasks. Indecision wastes your time and that of others.

Indecision and delay are major time wasters at work. They can have enormous costs in terms of lost money and lost time. You must learn how to deal with them effectively.

THE FOUR TYPES OF DECISIONS

∎

There are four types of decisions that you will have to deal with on a regular basis in the course of your career:

1. There are decisions that *only you* can make. This is the decision that no one else can make, and it is the decision that is your responsibility to make. It is therefore unavoidable.

2. There are decisions *you can delegate*. Some decisions can be made by someone else. One of the best ways to develop other people—to build knowledge, foresight, wisdom, and judgment in your subordinates, and in your children for that matter—is to allow them to make important decisions.

3. There are decisions that are *unaffordable*. The negative consequences of this decision are too great if it turns out poorly. Some decisions, if they turn out wrong, can lead to the bankruptcy of a company or to major losses. Some commitments of resources can be so serious that they become irretrievable. This is a decision that you cannot afford to make.

4. There are decisions that are *unavoidable.* Such a decision may require you to act on an opportunity for which delay could be expensive. The positive upside for you or the organization can be enormous. But remember, when it is not necessary to decide, it is necessary not to decide.

We will deal in depth with problem solving in chapter 7.

ONE THING AT A TIME
■

In work time, when you are working with and around other people, remember that you can do only one thing at a time. That one thing should be the most important thing that you can do at this minute.

There is a principle called the *Law of the Excluded Alternative.* This law states that whenever you choose to do one thing, you are simultaneously choosing not to do everything else that you could be doing at that moment. The reason this law is so important is that, quite often, the task you are choosing *not* to do is far more valuable and important than the task that you are

Master your time, master your life

working on right now. It has much greater potential consequences.

The most important quality for success at work is your ability to avoid distractions and time wasters. It is to keep focused on getting the most important results that you are responsible for.

Your ability to work efficiently and well in and around other people is absolutely essential to your success. You must think about how you can achieve this all the time.

<<< ACTION EXERCISES >>>

1. Work all the time you work; resolve today to minimize or eliminate the time wasters that contribute nothing to your life or work.

2. Leave things off; discipline yourself to use e-mail and text messaging quickly and efficiently, and then get back to work.

3. Plan your meetings, one-on-one and with groups, so that you accomplish the very most in the shortest period of time.

6

CREATIVE TIME

We have been endowed with the
capacity and the power to create
desirable pictures within and to
find them automatically printed in
the outer world of our
environment.

—JOHN McDONALD

Creative time is some of the most important and valuable time that you can ever spend. One idea can change your life and make you rich, and the better you plan and prepare for this idea, the more likely it is that you will have it. But creativity requires that you back away from the business of daily life in order to let your mind function at a higher level. This is why creative time requires a different form of thinking and organizing than work time or productive time.

It is said that every change in your life comes as the result of your mind colliding with a new idea. There seems to be a direct relationship between the number of ideas that you come up with, or are exposed to, and the likelihood that you will find exactly the right idea, at the right time, that can change your life completely and even make you rich.

It is estimated that each person has four ideas each year, any one of which would make them a millionaire if they followed up on it. How many times have you seen someone come out with a new product or service and go on to become wealthy? You say, "I thought of that idea a long time ago!"

Yes, you did. But you failed to act. You didn't do anything about the idea. As a result, someone else came up with the same idea and ran with it, trying it out, debugging it as she went along, and eventually making the new idea work at a high level. You could have done the same.

THE BILLION DOLLAR IDEA
■

In June 2009, my wife, my daughter, and I attended an all-day meeting with our publisher at their offices in downtown San Francisco. The meeting ended at 5:00. We were tired and looking forward to getting back to our hotel.

But when we walked out onto the sidewalks of San Francisco, there were no taxis. We walked a block to a busy intersection, looking for a taxi and waving at any taxi that went past, but no one stopped.

We walked another block to a hotel entrance, hoping to take a taxi from the taxi stand in front. But the taxi stand was empty. We walked for half an hour through the busy, teeming rush-hour traffic of San Francisco and could not find a single taxi to take us back to our hotel.

Eventually, tired and hungry, we stopped at a restaurant and had dinner. After dinner, we once more began our walk toward our hotel, which was a mile away, up the steep hills of San Francisco. This time, we finally found a taxi and made it back to our hotel.

We learned later that the unionized taxi industry had installed what is called "changeover time." This is the period between 5:00 P.M. and 7:00 P.M., when people need taxis more than almost any other time in the day. But this is when the taxi drivers go home for dinner. They shut off their lights and refuse to pick up anyone during that two-hour period.

THE IMPORTANCE OF TAKING ACTION

■

Here's the interesting part: In that same year, four other businessmen in San Francisco came out of a late meeting and tried to hail a taxicab. They had the same experience that we had had. They could not find a taxi anywhere. They ended up having to walk a considerable distance to get back to their hotels as well. They asked, as we did, "Why isn't it possible to get a taxi at rush hour, or at other times, in a big city like this?"

But while my family went back to the hotel, complaining and grumbling, those four businessmen decided to start a new company to fill this need. They saw a business opportunity to solve the problem of nonavailability of cabs. They called it Uber. They decided to make taxis available to anyone through a simple app that you could download for free. Today, the Uber concept has swept the world. As of 2016, the company was valued at $62.5 billion!

By the way, I had the same experience trying to find a taxi between 5:00 and 7:00 P.M. in both New York and Paris over the following two years. During those hours, the taxi industry simply shuts down. When Uber became available in New York and Paris, the taxi drivers revolted and went on strike. In Paris, they started riots and burned the cars of Uber drivers. Today, Uber has more cars and drivers in those two cities than the entire taxi industry had developed in the last hundred years. And they are all thriving.

YOU ARE A POTENTIAL GENIUS
∎

My point is this: There are great ideas all around you. All you need is one good idea to improve an existing product or to create a new product or service for you to begin your fortune.

Albert Einstein wrote, "Every child is born a genius."

The fact is that you were born a *potential* genius. You have the ability to solve almost any problem, overcome almost any obstacle, and achieve almost any goal that you can set for yourself, as long as you are clear about the goal, and you both focus and concentrate all of your mental energies on one idea at a time, like a laser beam.

The most important requirement of all for you to activate the full powers of your creative mind is *clarity*. You must be absolutely clear about the goal you want to achieve or the obstacle that stands in your way. The greater clarity you have, the faster you will attract into your life the ideas, people, and resources that you need to solve your problem or achieve your goal.

TYPES OF CREATIVITY

∎

There are two main types of creative intelligence: integrated intelligence and original thought.

With integrated intelligence, you combine and recombine existing information, ideas, and experience into new, better, and more desirable forms. This is why most creative breakthroughs come from people with considerable knowledge and experience in a particular field.

The second form of intelligence, original thought, is

when you come up with an idea no one else has thought of before. This idea may be based on a tremendous amount of knowledge and experience, but you take it to a higher level and you create something completely new, like Google, the iPhone, or Uber.

The wonderful discovery is that your creative ability is like a muscle. The more you use it, the stronger it becomes and the faster it works for you. By practicing some of the techniques described here, you can actually increase your IQ by as much as twenty-five points, moving you from average or above average into the genius range of intelligence.

WHAT HOLDS YOU BACK

If everyone has the capacity to function at genius levels, why is it that so few people ever unlock their full mental potential to come up with great ideas to change and improve their life or work?

There are three main enemies of creative thought: the *comfort zone*, *learned helplessness*, and *fear of failure or rejection*.

Perhaps the biggest enemy of progress is the comfort zone, a feeling of complacency or comfort that people get into after having done things in a certain way for a long period of time, or often for just a short period of time. This is why many of the great breakthroughs in business and technology are from new companies outside the industry and are started by people without the heavy baggage of past experience. They have no comfort zone to break out of.

The natural tendency is for a person to slip into a comfort zone and then to resist anything new or different in that area. Instead of being open to newer, better, faster, cheaper, or more convenient ways of producing the product or delivering the service, the average person resists change of any kind. They say things like, "We've always done it this way," or "We tried that once before and it didn't work," or "It costs too much," or "What's wrong with the way we're doing it now?"

In many companies, they have the *NIH syndrome*— not invented here. When somebody comes up with a new idea from outside of the industry, it is immediately rejected and dismissed.

FAILURE TO MOVE OUT OF THE COMFORT ZONE
■

In 2006, Apple announced the release of their new iPhone. You could activate the phone with a single button, type right on the phone's surface, take and send pictures and movies to your friends, communicate with social media, and download music instantly from the iTunes store.

It was revolutionary. People lined up and slept in the streets to buy the first phones available. Apple sold millions of the iPhones, and as of May 2016, has sold more than 947.7 million units and gone on to become the most valuable company in history.

In 2006, Nokia had 50 percent of the world consumer cell phone market. BlackBerry had 49 percent of the world business cell phone market. The executives of both of these companies, probably reading off the same script, said, "The iPhone is just a toy. It is a passing fad. People are not interested in all those bells and whistles. They will soon come back to the solid, dependable cell phones that we offer."

Within five years, both companies had gone from world leaders to closing their doors. They had become so complacent with their success that they could not change. BlackBerry even reduced its research and development budget by 50 percent because "they were so popular that they did not need to innovate anymore." This is how dangerous falling into a comfort zone can be, both in business and in personal life.

LEARNED HELPLESSNESS
■

The second enemy of creativity is learned helplessness. People feel helpless in the face of rapid change, competitive actions, or unexpected setbacks. This is one of the most common reasons people do not try something new or different. And if they think of an idea to do things in a different way, they immediately reject it and go back to what they were doing before.

Learned helplessness occurs when someone tries new ideas and fails, which young people do over and over again. After failing several times, and sometimes even after a single failure, they conclude that they cannot change the situation or the way things are. They develop learned helplessness and stop trying to do or try new things at all. This can happen very early in life and then persists throughout a person's career.

FEAR HOLDS YOU BACK
■

The third enemy of creativity is the fear of failure and its twin, the fear of rejection. The fear of failure triggers a form of paralysis, like a deer caught in the headlights. Whenever someone thinks that they might lose their time or lose their money, the fear of failure looms in their thinking, and they begin thinking about everything that could go wrong. They immediately back away from trying or investing in anything new or different.

In addition, the fear of rejection, caused by the fear of criticism, is a major reason people do not try new things. Many people are so sensitive to the possible negative opinions of others that they refuse to do anything new or different that might generate disapproval.

Whenever you have or hear a new idea, be alert to the natural tendency to resist the new idea by slipping back into your comfort zone, feeling incapable of making it work, or fearing failure or rejection.

The good news is that you can go from being uncreative to being extremely creative in almost no time at all. There are a series of methods and techniques to unlock your creativity that I have taught to more than two million people in seventy-five countries. People often tell me that one or more of these ideas had transformed their life and often made them wealthy.

ASK THE RIGHT QUESTIONS
∎

Here are four questions that you can ask yourself repeatedly. Each of these questions expands your thinking and enables you to see things you might not have seen before.

1. What are we trying to do? Ask this question especially when you are experiencing resistance or are not getting the results you expected. Become absolutely clear about what you are trying to accomplish. Has your goal changed?

2. How are we trying to do it? There are many different ways to achieve any goal. It is highly likely that the way you are attempting to achieve your goal is not the best way. The only real question is, Does it work? Is your current method working? The rule is to be clear about the goal but flexible about the method of achieving it.

3. What are our assumptions? If you are experiencing frustration, resistance, or temporary failure, ask yourself, What are my assumptions about this situation?

4. What if your assumptions were wrong? What would you do then?

Peter Drucker wrote, "Errant assumptions lay at the root of every failure."

ANALYZE YOUR ASSUMPTIONS
■

Each person has two types of assumptions, explicit and implicit. Explicit assumptions are those that you are conscious of and that you can clearly explain and defend to another person.

The first and most dangerous explicit assumption that a person makes in a new business is that there is an actual market for the product or service. But according to *Forbes* magazine, fully 80 percent of business failure is caused by a single factor: Customers simply do not want the product that you are offering.

Even with the best market research, fully 80 percent of new products introduced each year fail in the marketplace and have to be discontinued, costing enormous amounts of money. The people who developed and marketed the product proceeded on the assumption that there was a market demand for what they were selling and that the demand was big enough and profitable enough to justify all of the efforts to bring the product to market in the first place.

The second type of assumption is implicit, or unconscious. This is something that you believe without question. What could they be for you?

One fatal implicit assumption is, *Because I want to, I can.* Many people assume that their desire or willpower or determination is all that is necessary to overcome obstacles and eventually succeed. But there is often very little relationship between what you want to do and what you are capable of doing.

Another fatal assumption is, *Because I have to, I can.* The truth is that you may lack the knowledge, skills, money, or resources to achieve a particular goal that you feel is essential to your success.

Your life is greatly influenced by your assumptions. You always act on the basis of what you believe to be true, even if it is not true at all or you have no proof.

CHALLENGE YOUR ASSUMPTIONS
■

Be prepared to consider that your most cherished assumptions about yourself or your business could be completely wrong. This is a difficult possibility for most people to deal with. But whenever you are struggling to make progress in any area or facing what seems to be an unsolvable problem or difficulty, stand back and ask yourself, What if I am completely wrong in what I am trying to do?

What if we are completely wrong in our current approach? What if there is a completely different way to achieve this goal? What if we could do something that has never been done before (Uber!)? The words *what if?* are probably responsible for more creative breakthroughs than any other words.

Edward de Bono, an expert on thinking styles, calls this "PO," or provocation operation. Like an electric cattle prod. Whenever you ask a provocative question that challenges or shakes up your thinking, you stimulate creativity and creative responses.

Could there be a better way? This is a great question that can sometimes make you rich. The fact is that there is always a better way for you to solve any problem or accomplish any goal. There is always a better way to produce, sell, or deliver any product or service.

Practice *reinvention*. Imagine that you are starting your business or career over again today, with everything that you now know. Imagine your business burned to the ground and you could walk across the street and start again with no baggage from the past. What would you do differently? What would you start doing or stop doing? What changes would you make immediately?

The exercise of reinvention can free you from the comfort zone of the past and open up your mind to all kinds of new possibilities.

UNLOCKING YOUR CREATIVITY
■

There are four ways you can solve any problem, make any change, or achieve any goal:

1. You can do *more of* certain things. What should you be doing more of? Answer: You should be doing more of those things that are giving you the very best results today. What are they?

2. You can do *less of* other things. And what should you be doing less of? Answer: You should be doing less of those things that are not working very well or not working at all.

3. You can *start* doing something completely new or different. This is the hardest step of all, but usually doing something new or different is the step that leads to the greatest breakthroughs in every field. What should you start doing today that you are not now doing?

4. You can *stop* doing certain things altogether. And what should you stop doing? You should stop doing anything that is not helping you to achieve your most important goals. Use the A/B Method described in chapter 1.

THINK ON PAPER
∎

There is something miraculous that happens between the head and the hand. When you write something down on a piece of paper, you trigger what is called a *psychoneuromotor* activity. This is a big word for activating your whole brain into focusing on a single point for a period of time. When you write, you think, visualize, and move simultaneously. It is not possible for you to write and at the same time think or pay attention to anything else in the world except what you are writing at that moment.

Because your mind and body are completely engaged, when you write something down, it is automatically transferred to your subconscious mind. Writing things down dramatically increases the likelihood that you will remember them. Writing down your goals increases the likelihood that you will achieve them. Writing things down activates your creative ability. It stimulates your brain. It is like stepping on the accelerator of your mental engine.

SOLVE ANY PROBLEM

■

Here is a simple exercise for you. Select a problem that you have been trying to solve. Take a clean sheet of paper and write out every detail of this problem. Write down all the facts or information you have about this situation.

Ask questions like these: What am I trying to do? How am I trying to do it? What exactly is the problem or goal? How did this problem arise? When did it happen or occur for the first time? Who was involved? Why did this problem happen? Is this really a problem or could it be an opportunity? These questions stimulate your creativity.

You will be amazed at what you think of when you begin writing, line after line, every detail of the problem you are wrestling with, including all the possible causes and the many possible solutions. Sometimes during this exercise, the exact right idea or solution will jump off the page at you.

I have worked with people who had been struggling with a goal or problem for many months who were able to solve it in a few minutes by simply taking the time, in the quiet, to write down every detail of the problem. As a result, the problem practically solved itself on the paper in front of them.

YOUR SUPERCONSCIOUS MIND
∎

Throughout history, people have talked and written about a higher form of mind or thinking that each person has available to them. Sigmund Freud called it the "superego." Alfred Adler called it the "supraconscious mind." Napoleon Hill referred it to as "infinite intelligence." Ralph Waldo Emerson called it the "over-soul." Many people refer to it as the "God mind." After many years of research, I prefer to call it *the superconscious mind*.

However you describe it, this mind is always available to you, just as is your iPhone or laptop computer. You can turn it on and access it at any time. In a few moments, all of your superconscious powers become available to you to solve your problems and achieve your goals.

ACTIVATING YOUR MENTAL POWERS
∎

The superconscious mind has several amazing qualities:

1. The superconscious mind will enable you to achieve any goal you want as long as the goal

is clear. People who write and rewrite and think about their goals constantly seem to enjoy a steady stream of ideas that help them achieve their goals faster.

2. The superconscious mind has access to all your previous knowledge and experience, from throughout your entire life; plus it has access to the knowledge and experience of others, even at a great distance.

3. The superconscious mind is the seat of the power of attraction. When you have a clear goal, the superconscious mind sends out vibrations that turn you into a "living magnet." With this power, you begin to attract into your life the ideas, people, circumstances, and money that you need you to achieve your goals.

4. The superconscious mind automatically solves every problem on the way to the goal, as long as the goal is clear.

5. The superconscious mind will bring you exactly the answer you need, at exactly the right time. But this information is "time dated." You must act on it immediately in some way, or it will be too late.

6. Your superconscious mind will bring you the lessons you need to achieve your goal, often

disguised as obstacles, setbacks, and temporary failure. Your main job is to look into the
problem or difficulty and ask, What can I
learn from this experience?

7. When the superconscious mind brings you
   the answer that you need, it will be complete
   in every respect and always within your current capabilities. You will be able to take action on your idea immediately. The answer
   will feel simple, logical, and clear, like a
   blinding flash of the obvious.

Your superconscious mind often speaks to you
through your intuition, "the still, small voice within." If
you listen to your intuition and follow its guidance,
you'll probably never make another mistake.

Fortunately, your superconscious mind is always available, even if you have not paid attention to it, or listened
to your intuition, for a long time. It actually grows stronger and works faster as you use it and trust in it.

MIND STORMING
■

There is another way that you can use the power of pen
and paper to activate your subconscious and supercon-

scious minds. It is called the *20 Ideas Method.* More people have become wealthy with this method than any other practical way of creative thinking ever discovered. It also activates your superconscious mind.

Here is how it works: Take a clean sheet of paper and write your most important goal at the top of the page in the form of a question. For example, you could write, "How can I double my income over the next twelve months, or by such and such a date?"

Even better, select a specific amount. Write, "How can I earn $XX,XXX by this specific date?"

The question must be simple and clear, something that a six-year-old child could understand and that triggers practical answers, as this question does.

You then discipline yourself to write down at least twenty answers to your question. But here is a warning: The first time you do this, you will find that it is one of the hardest thinking exercises that you have ever practiced.

Your first three to five answers will be simple and obvious—do more of this or less of that. Your next three to five answers will be more difficult. What should you start doing or stop doing?

The next ten answers will be some of the most difficult of your life. Unless you exert tremendous discipline, you will feel like giving up and quitting this exercise. This is normal and natural the first time that you practice mind storming.

KEEP WRITING
■

But if you discipline yourself to continue writing until you have written out a minimum of twenty answers, something amazing will happen. Very often, among those answers will be a breakthrough idea that enables you to achieve your goal, or starts you off in a new direction that leads you to the right solution.

You can use mind storming as a regular part of your life. Every time you have a goal, sit down with a sheet of paper, write the goal as a question at the top of the page, and then write twenty answers to your question.

The final part of mind storming is for you to take action immediately on at least one of the ideas you have generated. When you take action on one of these ideas, you keep your creative juices flowing. Taking action on one idea triggers additional ideas. Taking action on an idea activates your superconscious mind and begins to attract into your life people and circumstances that can help you.

BRAINSTORMING

■

The brainstorming method, developed by advertising executive Alex Osborn in 1946, has become one of the most popular creative thinking techniques of all, often leading to breakthrough results.

When you bring a group of people together to focus their intelligence and creativity on a single problem or goal, you activate and stimulate the minds of everyone in the group. A higher mind then becomes available to all the participants, often triggering ideas that nobody had thought of before.

Brainstorming is simple. There are a few basic rules that you can practice in your first brainstorming session.

1. The ideal group size for a brainstorming session is four to six people. Fewer than four people is not enough to get the full value of brainstorming, and more than six people does not give each person a chance to share their best thinking.

2. A brainstorming session should be fifteen to forty-five minutes long. Start and stop on time. When everyone is clear when the brainstorming session ends, like the final bell at

the stock exchange, more ideas will be stimulated in a shorter period of time.

3. Here's the key: No criticism. No ridicule. No judgment at all of any of the ideas. The leader of the brainstorming session remains totally positive, complimenting every idea and praising people for their contributions.

4. Focus on quantity of ideas rather than quality. Make it a game to see how many different ideas, no matter how ridiculous, the group can generate within the specific time prescribed.

5. The job of the leader is to encourage everyone to contribute their best ideas, especially those participants who might be a little shy or reserved. Often, these quieter people have incredible ideas if they get a chance to share them.

6. Assign one person the job of keeping notes. Record each idea. Write it down. Afterward, you can type up all the ideas for review or circulation. Sometimes, one good brainstorming session can change the direction of a company or a life.

7. Encourage the participants to come back to you later if they think of any ideas that did

not come up in the brainstorming session. Remember, one new idea, if it is the right idea at the right time, can be all you need to transform your results.

THE FIVE-STEP CREATIVE THINKING PROCESS
■

The starting point of unlocking your creative genius to achieve any goal is *clarity*. This requires that you *verbalize* or express your goal clearly in words. The simplest way to do this is to simply write down your goal in the present tense, beginning with the word *I*, followed by an action verb.

When you say, "I achieve this particular goal by this particular time," your subconscious and superconscious minds accept this as a command and begin working on this goal twenty-four hours a day.

The second step to unlocking your creativity is for you to *visualize*. Create a clear mental picture of your goal as if it were already a reality. There is a direct relationship between how clearly you can see your goal in your mind's eye and how rapidly you achieve it.

The third step is for you to *emotionalize* your goal. "Get the feeling."

Imagine and create the feeling that you would enjoy if you achieved your goal exactly as you have verbalized and visualized it. Create within yourself the feelings of joy, satisfaction, happiness, relief, or personal pride that you will experience when you achieve this goal. These three techniques—verbalization, visualization, and emotionalization—activate your creative mind and unlock your mental powers.

The fourth stage is for you to practice complete *relaxation*. Let it go completely. Get your mind busy elsewhere. Forget about the goal and become so busy doing something else that you don't think about it at all. During this time, your superconscious mind will be working on your goal nonstop.

The fifth stage is *realization*. This occurs when exactly the answer or insight that you need appears in your mind, complete in every respect.

These five steps—verbalization, visualization, emotionalization, relaxation, and realization—are the keys to your becoming one of the most creative people in your world.

You are a potential genius. Even if you have not used your incredible mental capabilities for a long time, you can stimulate them immediately by doing the things we've talked about in this chapter. There are no limits to what you can accomplish when you unlock your full creative potential.

<<< ACTION EXERCISES >>>

1. Develop absolute clarity about the goal of success and wealth that you would like to achieve. Create a clear mental picture of what your life and work would look like when you achieve this goal.

2. Gather information that can help you achieve this goal. The more new ideas you come up with, the more likely it is that you will discover the exact idea you need at exactly the right time.

3. Set aside times of silence and reflection during which your superconscious mind can work to bring you exactly the answer you need.

7

PROBLEM-SOLVING AND DECISION-MAKING TIME

I have learned that success is to be
measured not so much by the
position that one has reached in life
as by the obstacles which he has
overcome while trying to succeed.

—BOOKER T. WASHINGTON

All of life is a series of problems and difficulties, set-backs and failures. Every hour, every day, you make decisions that affect your life in major and minor ways. Solving problems and making decisions requires a particular type of thinking and approach. It requires a special way of using your time and your intelligence.

Your ability to solve problems and make decisions is one of the most critical determinants of your success at work or in life. In fact, you will rise to the height of your abilities to solve the problems that you meet at your current level every hour of every day.

A goal unachieved is merely a problem unsolved. The only thing that stands between you and anything you want in life is an obstacle or a difficulty of some kind. Your ability to remove this obstacle or overcome this difficulty determines how much you are paid and how fast you will be promoted.

THE UNIVERSAL PRINCIPLE
■

The universal principle is, *You become what you think about most of the time.*

Successful people, the top 10 or 20 percent of people in our society, tend to think very differently from the bottom 80 or 90 percent. Top people think about their goals most of the time. They think about where they are going and what they want to accomplish most of the time. Especially, the most successful people think and talk about solutions to the inevitable and unavoidable problems that they face every single day.

What do unhappy, unsuccessful people think and talk about? They think and talk about their problems, and who is to blame.

Successful people think about the solutions and the actions that they can take immediately to begin moving forward toward the things that they want.

The rule is, What you think about, you bring about. Whatever you dwell on grows in your reality. If you think and talk about your problems, they increase and multiply. But when you think and talk about solutions, you continuously discover more and better solutions.

THINK IN TERMS OF ACTION
∎

Whenever you have a problem of any kind, immediately ask the questions, What can be done? and What is our next action?

In problem solving, as in other areas, clarity is your best friend. When you are absolutely clear about the goal you want to achieve, it is easier for you develop clarity about the things that are stopping you from achieving that goal. When you have absolute clarity about the things that you need to do to get the things that you want, you can focus and concentrate single-mindedly on doing just those things that can help you the most.

Here are two questions for you. First, ask, What are the three biggest problems in my life today?

These are the problems that you think about most of the time. They are the major barriers to your success and happiness.

Then ask, What are the three best solutions to each of these problems?

Sometimes these simple questions help you solve the problems and make the necessary decisions quickly and easily. Often, the correct solutions are clear and obvious. You just need to open your eyes.

In the 13th century, Sir William of Occam put forth

what has become known as Occam's razor. This law says that the most likely solution to any problem is the simplest of all solutions available. Even earlier, Socrates said that the correct solution is usually the solution that contains the fewest possible steps.

What are the simplest solutions to your most pressing problems? Sometimes they are so clear and simple that you are amazed that you have not seen them before.

CONSTRAINT THEORY

■

Israeli management consultant Eliyahu Goldratt developed the "theory of constraints" as a business principle some years ago. It is now taught and used all over the world. There are even three-day seminars during which executives are trained to apply these principles to solving problems; removing obstacles; and getting more done, faster, under any circumstances.

The theory itself is quite simple. It begins with your becoming clear about your goal. Where are you now and what do you want to achieve?

In business, your goal could be a certain level of sales, growth, profitability, market share, or cost reduction.

Whatever your goal, you then ask the key question: What is the limiting factor, or constraint, that sets the speed at which I achieve this goal?

Another way to ask this question is: Why aren't I already at my goal?

Do you want to double your income? Well, why isn't your income already twice as high?

QUESTION YOUR CONSTRAINTS
■

Many people make up elaborate excuses to justify and explain why they have not achieved the things they really want in life. They then fall in love with their excuses. No matter what the difficulty or problem they are having in achieving their business or personal goals, they roll out a steady stream of excuses to absolve themselves of taking effective action.

When you ask the question, Why aren't I already at my goal? your favorite excuses will jump out at you. You will immediately think of all the reasons you use for achieving less than you really want.

Why isn't your income already twice as high? The real reason is probably because your ability to get results that people will pay you for is not high enough.

Why aren't you already at your ideal weight? It is almost always because you eat too much and exercise too little.

Whenever you hide behind an excuse, trotting it out and giving it to yourself and others, you shut down your problem-solving capabilities. You engage in "learned helplessness."

Here is a way to test if your excuses are valid. Ask, Is there any person or organization that has the same problems and difficulties that I have that is achieving their goals nonetheless?

Is there anyone in your field who is earning twice as much as you? Is there anyone who is younger than you who may have less education or have had fewer opportunities in life, but who is doing better than you? If your answer is yes, then your excuse has no foundation in fact. It is not true. It is a deception that you have talked yourself into but which is contradicted by the reality of the world around you.

ASSUME THERE IS ALWAYS A SOLUTION
■

If you want to unlock your full potential, you must avoid the fatal disease of "excusitis." This is an inflammation of the excuse-making gland, which is invariably fatal to success.

Begin by assuming that for any problem or difficulty there is an answer or a solution just waiting to be found. Your absolute confidence that there is a solution and that you can find it makes you positive, confident, and more likely to solve the problem.

Solving problems and making decisions is what you do in your life and work all day long. No matter what job description is written on your business card, your true job is "Problem Solver."

Your success and promotion are largely determined by your demonstrated ability to solve the problems that you meet at your current level.

Henry Kissinger once said, "The only reward you get for solving problems is even larger problems to solve."

The bigger and more complex the problems you can solve, the more valuable and important you become to your organization, and the more you will be paid. The most highly respected and successful people in any company are those who can solve the biggest and most complex problems.

FOCUS ON THE SOLUTION

■

Your ability to focus on a single problem or decision is very important to your success. The same amount of electricity necessary to power a lightbulb, properly focused into a laser beam, will cut through steel. When you focus all of your attention on solving a particular problem, or achieving a particular goal, your mind becomes more and more like a laser beam, capable of cutting through any obstacle that stands in your way.

You can dramatically improve your ability to solve problems by asking and answering the right questions over and over again. When I conducted problem-solving and decision-making seminars for IBM some years ago, I always began by encouraging the participants to ask a series of key questions.

Question number one is, Exactly what is the problem that you are dealing with right now?

The biggest obstacle to solving problems is lack of clarity about exactly what the problem is in the first place.

Question number two is, Is this really a problem or could it be an opportunity?

Many of the greatest breakthroughs in business and science came about as the results of a product, service, or experiment that failed completely. This failure revealed new information or forced people to do something completely different from what they had started off to do. And in that new direction was incredible success.

THE GREAT BREAKTHROUGH
∎

One of the greatest medical breakthroughs of the twentieth century was the discovery of penicillin by Sir Alexander Fleming in a laboratory experiment that failed. In 1928, Fleming had put some bacteria on agar in a glass dish and then gone out for lunch. When he got back he was disappointed to find that all of the bacteria in his experiment had died completely. Whereas the typical researcher would have simply thrown away the tainted agar and begun again, Fleming instead asked, "What kind of substance was so powerful that it could kill all this bacteria so quickly?"

He found that an experiment with a new spore in another part of the laboratory had been left uncovered, allowing spores to drift through the air and fall in different parts of the lab, including on the bacteria in Fleming's agar dish. This spore was eventually isolated and named penicillin, the most powerful antibiotic ever discovered. In World War II, a decade later, penicillin saved millions of lives from disease and infection.

As a result of this discovery, Fleming was knighted by the king of England, won the Nobel Prize in medicine, became very wealthy, and was heralded as one of the most respected and esteemed doctors in British history. He still is today.

EXPAND YOUR DEFINITION
∎

Once you have a clear definition of the problem, you ask yourself the magic question: What *else* is the problem? The rule is to beware of a problem for which there is only one definition. It seems that the more ways you can define and restate the problem, the more likely you are to arrive at the right definition, which will lead to the correct solution. Take your time.

The next question you ask is, What is the best solution to this problem?

Once you have determined the best solution, ask, What *else* might be a solution? Again, beware of a problem for which there is only one solution. Keep asking, What else is the solution?

A major obstacle to problem solving is jumping to conclusions and making decisions before you have even considered all the other possibilities. The more solutions you can develop, including doing nothing at all, before you move to a decision, the more likely it is that you will come up with the ideal solution. There seems to be a direct relationship between the *quantity* of problem definitions and solutions you can develop and the *quality* of the final solution you settle on.

MIND STORMING REVISITED
■

Practice the mind storming method explained in the previous chapter to develop more solutions quickly. Write your definition of the problem at the top of a page in the form of a question, "How can we solve this problem or achieve this goal?"

You then discipline yourself to write at least twenty answers to your question. The more solutions you can generate, simply by the *law of probabilities*, the more likely it is that you will generate the correct solution, which will lead to the breakthrough that you desire. Take your time.

A 500 PERCENT INCREASE
■

Some years ago, I conducted the following exercise with the senior executives of a $20 million company. They had worked for more than twenty years to achieve this level of sales and revenues. Their question was, How can we double our sales over the next five years?

We then spent the next hour writing out all the different ways they could overcome the obstacles of competition and the challenges of rapid change to achieve this goal. We then organized the ideas by priority and

MASTER YOUR TIME, MASTER YOUR LIFE

determined which ones were inputs and which ones were outputs, or results.

Finally, we assigned specific responsibility for each of these tasks to different individuals and set deadlines for the completion of each job. Then everyone went back to work.

Five years later, they invited me to a special banquet to celebrate their best year ever. But instead of doubling their sales in five years, by applying many of the new ideas they had generated, they increased their sales to $105 million! They became a market leader and remain the market leader in their field even today.

ASSIGN RESPONSIBILITY

∎

Once you have clearly identified the true problem that you are attempting to solve and have agreed on the best solution, the next question is, Who is going to be responsible for carrying out this solution?

It is amazing how many problem-solving meetings end with a clear, agreed-upon solution, but two weeks later the problem still exists. Why? Because no one was assigned specific responsibility for implementing the solution.

When you have chosen a specific person to be responsible for the solution, set measures that you can use to determine progress, and to ensure that the solution has been successful. Set deadlines and subdeadlines. The more important the solution is to your company or to you personally, the more regularly you should check to make sure that everything is being done on time and on budget.

THE PETER PRINCIPLE

■

Some years ago, a man named Dr. Laurence Peter wrote a book called *The Peter Principle*. This became a bestseller and an eye-opener for millions of people. Peter said, "Each person in an organization is continually promoted based on their ability to do their job and get results. This promotion process continues until the employee reaches the level where he can no longer do his job in a satisfactory manner. At that point, he stops being promoted. His career levels out."

For this reason, Peter said, "Eventually each person rises to their level of incompetence."

His critical insight was that people who have reached their level of incompetence eventually staff every large organization at every level. They are not capable of doing their work well at that level, or of being promoted or demoted. All organizations, but especially government organizations, end up being staffed by incompetent people. This insight explains a lot of the problems with underperformance and excessive spending in government bureaucracies.

YOUR PROBLEM-SOLVING ABILITY

This is what happens in your life as well. When you start your career, you are given work to do requiring that you solve problems and achieve results at that level. As you demonstrate a mastery of your work, by solving the problems, overcoming the obstacles, and getting the results expected of you, you are promoted, almost automatically, to more responsible positions.

At each new position, the problems you face will be more difficult and more complex and will have greater consequences for success or failure. As you demonstrate your ability to solve the more difficult problems at that level, you will be automatically promoted again and again. Your ability to solve problems and achieve results determines how high you rise and how far you go in your career.

BECOME SOLUTION ORIENTED

∎

Develop an intense solution orientation. The more you think about solutions, the more solutions you will discover. The more confident you become that you can solve any problem you face, the more likely it is that you will find the right solution at the right time for you.

Identify your biggest problems in life today. Think about the steps you could take immediately to solve them. Then take continuous action toward the solution of your problems and the achievement of your goals.

Problem-solving and decision-making time can be done two ways. The first is when you sit quietly by yourself with a pad of paper, focusing single-mindedly on one problem at a time and writing down all the ideas that come to you.

The second way is when you collaborate with one or more people to focus on a single problem or obstacle. These two activities are more important for your success than anything else you do.

Problem-solving and decision-making time, if you plan and use them correctly, can do more to help you advance in your career than almost any other activity you can engage in.

<<< ACTION EXERCISES >>>
---

1. What is the biggest single problem you are wrestling with today? Define it in writing.

2. Write it at the top of a page in the form of a question beginning with "How can we solve this problem?"

3. Discipline yourself, alone or with others, to generate twenty different ways to solve this problem. Take action immediately on at least one answer.

8

PEOPLE AND FAMILY TIME

You will find as you look back
upon your life that the moments
that stand out, the moments when
you have really lived, are the
moments when you have done
things in a spirit of love.

—HENRY DRUMMOND

The time you spend with other people, and the way you spend it, determines perhaps 85 percent of your happiness, success, or failure in life.

People time is different from work time, productive time, creative time, and learning time. What you need to do to be effective and successful in your work and career is almost the opposite of what you need to do to be effective and successful with your family and relationships.

Harmonious relationships require large chunks of *unbroken* time, both at home and at work. In your career, the things you do and say in your interactions with others largely determines your future. More people are let go for personality problems than for lack of technical competence in every business and in every type of economy. At home, the quality of your relationships is more important than anything else.

In life, there is a simple equation: QR × QR = PS, or

the quantity of your relationships times the quality of those relationships equals your personal success.

At home, the people you love and the people who love you in return will determine the quality of your emotional life. Your choice of a spouse, mate, or companion will largely determine how happy and fulfilled you will be.

The only way to increase the value of a relationship is to invest more time into that relationship. There is a direct relationship between the quantity of time that you invest and the quality of the relationship that you will have with that other person. Nothing can replace time, and usually face-to-face time.

BALANCE IS ESSENTIAL

To be truly happy, you must achieve a balance between your family/relationships and your work life. But each of these activities requires a different type of time. Work requires *quality* time—setting goals and priorities, working on high-value activities, getting results, and performing at your best. Family time requires *quantity* time—long unbroken stretches of time where the happiest and most important moments of your life take place.

It is said that we live life by the days and months, but we experience it in the *moments*. The most important moments of your life, as you look back, occur almost always unbidden and unexpected, usually complete surprises. You could not have planned or prepared for them.

The essayist Michel de Montaigne wrote, "The greatest joys in life are happy memories, which you can revisit at any moment of time. Therefore, the great business of life is to create as many of them as possible."

You create memories by allowing large blocks of relaxed, unstructured time during which those unexpected memories can occur. And you never know when they will happen.

AS WITHIN, SO WITHOUT

■

A major purpose of working to become successful in your career is so that you can enjoy a higher standard and quality of life with the people who are most important to you. You will be truly happy only when your behavior on the outside is congruent, or in harmony, with your values on the inside. Lack of congruence, allowing your life to get out of balance, is a major source of stress and unhappiness as well as physical and mental illness.

Many people, especially men, say that their families are more important to them than anything else. They say the main reason they are working so hard is to provide a good life for their families. But then they work long hours, come home late, watch television when they do come home, and play golf on the weekends. Recent research says that the average father spends an average of eight minutes per day with each child.

This allocation of time can cause considerable stress. Just as a car vibrates and shakes when a wheel gets out of alignment, your life begins to vibrate and shake, to become unhappy and stressful, when it gets out of balance.

IMAGINE YOUR IDEAL LIFE
■

The starting point of getting your life into balance is for you to practice *idealization*. Imagine that you could wave a magic wand and make your family and personal life perfect in every respect. What would it look like? What kind of a lifestyle would you have? Where would you be living? Where would you be working? What would you be doing? What kind of people would you be living or working with? And how would your ideal life in the future be different from your current life today?

Practice zero-based thinking on your work and your

personal life. Ask the question, Is there anything that I am doing in my life that, knowing what I now know, I would not start up or get into again today?

Apply this question to your relationships, of all kinds. Is there any person in your life, personal or business, who, knowing what you now know, you would not get involved with again?

If the answer is yes, then your next question is simple: How do I get out of this situation and how fast?

It is amazing how many people are unhappy, stressed, and unfulfilled because they continue to remain in a relationship, which, knowing what they now know, based on their experiences, they would never enter into again if they had a chance.

What I have discovered is that if you would not enter into a relationship with someone again today, knowing what you now know, the relationship is *finished*. It is over. It cannot be saved. The only question now is: How long will you suffer and how much will you pay before you admit that the relationship is finished?

GET YOUR RELATIONSHIPS IN ORDER
∎

One of the very best uses of your time is to get your relationships in order. On a regular basis, examine each of your important relationships and ask the following questions:

> What should I be doing more of, if I want both of us to be happier?
>
> What should I be doing less of to improve the quality of this relationship?
>
> What should I start doing today that I am not doing now if I want to improve this relationship?
>
> What should I stop doing completely to improve the quality of this relationship?

Some years ago, after I discovered these questions, I went home and sat down with my wife and small children. I asked them what they would like me to do more of or less of to be a better husband and father. What would they like me to start doing or stop doing altogether to make them happier?

They didn't hesitate. They told me. They had several suggestions for me about things to do more of or less of or to start or to stop. I was quite amazed at how much room there was for improvement. I accepted their advice without arguing or defending and acted on it. It took a lot of courage, but it was one of the best family-building exercises I ever engaged in. Try it yourself and see.

WHAT IS REALLY IMPORTANT?

■

Here is a good way to improve the quality of your relationships and family life. Ask, What would I do, how would I spend my time, if I learned today that I only had six months left to live?

This is a great question. What would you do more of or less of? What would you start doing or stop doing? How would you spend your last six months on earth? Almost invariably your answer will revolve around the people in your life, making peace with people from the past and spending the rest of your time with those people who are most important to you.

Here's the rule: Whatever you would do if you learned that you only had a short time to live, you should start doing it *immediately*. You should incorporate your answer into your day-to-day life. Don't wait until it's too late.

BE FULLY PRESENT WITH YOUR FAMILY

■

The key to a happy life is to spend more time with your family. But what exactly does this mean? It means that when you are with your family, you are really there 100 percent of the time. Turn off the television and computer. Turn off your smartphone or put it on silent. Close the book you are reading and fold up the newspaper.

Eliminate all distractions. Focus single-mindedly on the other person, as if he were the most important person in the world. You are really with another person only when you are face to face, head to head, knee to knee, and heart to heart. You are really spending time with another person only when you are *in her face*. You are only fully engaged with her when you are talking to and with her, listening attentively to her responses, and paying complete attention to her.

When someone in your family or home wants to talk to you, stop whatever you are doing and concentrate single-mindedly on him or her and what he or she has to say. Make it clear to the other person that he/she is the most important person in the world at that moment.

TRUST AND LIKABILITY
■

The most important qualities for success with people, at work and at home, are trust and likability. As long as the other person likes and trusts you, the relationship can endure any number of problems and difficulties.

But if the trust and respect are lost, it is only a matter of time before the relationship collapses.

And here's the rule: *Listening builds trust.*

There is a direct relationship between how much and how well you listen and the level of warmth and trust you build with another person.

There are four keys to effective listening. When you practice these listening skills with each person you meet, you will be amazed at the results.

I. Listen Attentively

When a person speaks to you, immediately stop whatever you are doing. Face the person directly. Focus your eyes on her lips with occasional flicks to her eyes. Lean forward. Nod, smile, and be actively engaged in the words and conversation of the other person.

Above all, don't interrupt. When you interrupt a person when she is speaking, it is the same as sticking out your leg to trip someone who is walking down the sidewalk. Interrupting another person trips her emotionally. It makes her feel angry and frustrated. Interrupting someone immediately lowers the level of trust and warmth she might feel toward you.

Intense listening is the highest form of flattery. When you listen intensely to another person when she is speaking, your listening actually affects her emotionally and physically. Her heart rate increases; her self-esteem goes up. People like themselves more when you are listening intensely to them, and as a result they like you more as well.

2. Pause before Replying

When the other person stops speaking, remain silent for a few seconds, or longer. Resist the urge to immediately express your own ideas or opinions.

Most people do not listen to others; they simply wait politely until they can jump in with their own comments or observations. It is said, "Most conversation is not listening; it is just waiting." But when you pause before replying after the other person has stopped speaking, you achieve three marvelous benefits:

> First, you avoid the risk of interrupting the other person if she is just stopping to collect her thoughts before continuing.
>
> Second, you tell her, with your silence, that you really value what she is saying and by extension, you value her, by pausing and allowing silence to take place in the conversation.

Third, when you pause, you actually hear the other person at a deeper level of mind. You hear both what is said and what is not said, by allowing the other person's words to soak in for a few seconds.

3. Question for Clarification

Never assume that you understand exactly what the other person said or meant. If there is any question at all, simply smile and ask, "How do you mean?"

This is a magic question in any language. When you ask a person, How do you mean? the other person will always continue speaking and expand on what she had just said.

You can also ask, "How do you mean, exactly?"

The good thing about this question is that it is "invisible." You can ask it over and over again, and the other person will never hear the question itself. Instead, her mind will immediately focus on her answer, which she will give you as she continues speaking.

The rule is that *the person who asks questions has control.*

The person who is asking the questions controls the person who is answering the questions in a very subtle way. The secret to being charming in your conversations with others is for you to ask questions, smile, nod, listen intently, and react to the other person as if what she is saying were one of the most important and fascinating things that you have ever heard. The first time you try this, you will be astonished by the reaction of the other person.

4. Feed It Back

The fourth key to effective listening is for you to feed it back in your own words. Instead of responding immediately, ask something like, "Let me be sure I understand exactly what you just said. Did you mean this or that, or something else?"

This is called the *acid test of listening*. When you can feed back what a person has just said in your own words, paraphrasing her thoughts or ideas, you prove to her that you were really listening. As a result, she likes and respects you even more and is even more open to your influence.

CONNECT WITH OTHERS
■

The author of *Emotional Intelligence*, Daniel Goleman, said in a *Fortune* interview that the highest form of emotional intelligence, and the most helpful and important human quality, is *persuasiveness*. Successful people, in every area of life, are more persuasive than others. They have a wonderful ability to persuade others to cooperate with them and to go along with their ideas.

President Dwight D. Eisenhower once said, "The key to leadership is to get people to do what you want them to do and to think of it as their own idea."

The best way to become more persuasive is to ask well-thought-out and organized questions that bring people around to your point of view. Listening is perhaps the most powerful element of persuasion that you can practice.

SEVEN KEYS TO SUCCESS WITH PEOPLE
■

Dale Carnegie, in his best-selling book *How to Win Friends and Influence People*, said, "The deepest craving of human nature is the need to feel important."

Psychologists say that your level of self-esteem, how much you like and respect yourself, and how important and valuable you feel, lies at the core of your personality.

Your self-esteem determines how happy you feel about yourself and your relationships with others. Your level of self-esteem determines the goals that you set, and how persistent you are in achieving those goals. Your level of self-esteem determines how happy you are every single day.

There are seven ways you can make others feel important, raising their levels of self-esteem and self-confidence and making them feel happy about themselves.

I. Be Positive

Refuse to criticize, complain, or condemn anyone for any reason. Whenever you criticize others, for any reason, you lower their self-esteem, take away their self-respect, and undermine their self-confidence. Criticism, complaining, and condemnation make people feel angry and unhappy.

Destructive criticism experienced is the most hurtful of all behaviors. Destructive criticism in childhood is the main reason for most unhappiness and problems in adult life. Eliminate it from your vocabulary.

2. Be Agreeable

Being agreeable means that you never argue. Never tell people that they are wrong. This makes them angry and defensive. They shut down and become closed off to being influenced by you. By telling them that they are wrong, you diminish their self-esteem and make them resistant to any attempt by you to prove that they have made a mistake.

Instead, when someone says something with which you disagree, you can take control of the conversation by asking questions such as, Why do you say that? and Where did you hear that?

Instead of arguing, be curious. Ask people if they could help you understand their point of view. Practice your listening skills. Smile, nod, and pay attention.

In many cases, even if the person is completely wrong about a subject, it is not that important. Let it go. It doesn't really matter.

3. Practice Acceptance

One of the deepest subconscious needs of each person is to be accepted by others, just for the person he is, without any judgment or criticism. Many of the personal, political, and social problems we have nationwide and worldwide are caused by people who are shouting out to be accepted by others.

And how do you express acceptance? Simple. You smile whenever you meet a person. Whenever you smile, you tell others that you accept them unconditionally. You tell them that they are valuable and worthwhile. As a result, they like and accept themselves more. They feel happier about themselves and they feel happier toward you.

4. Express Appreciation

The two most magical words in any language are probably the words *thank you*. Whenever you thank another person for anything he has said or done, his self-esteem immediately goes up. He likes and respects himself more. He feels happier. He then becomes wide open to doing even more of those things that make you happy, causing you to thank him again.

5. Practice Admiration

Express your admiration for others at every opportunity. As Abraham Lincoln said, "Everybody likes a compliment."

Compliment people on their possessions, their accomplishments, and their personal traits. Compliment the host on what a beautiful house he has and how beautifully it is furnished. Compliment the businessman on his office and place of business. Compliment people for their accomplishments, their degrees and prizes. You can always find something to compliment, and when you do, you not only raise the self-esteem of the other person and make him feel important, but you feel better and happier about yourself as well.

6. Express Praise and Approval

Praise people for everything they do for you, large and small. One definition of self-esteem is how much a person feels *praiseworthy*. Your own self-esteem is determined by how worthy you feel of praise and respect from other people.

All of the striving in the world today after praise, approval, and rewards is to satisfy the deep human need for approval by other people. When you satisfy this need with each person you talk to, you raise his self-esteem and increase his desire to cooperate with you.

7. Pay Attention

Listen to others when they want to talk. When you pay attention to another person, you tell him without words that you consider him to be valuable and important. This is the magic of listening that we spoke about earlier.

You always pay attention to those people who you most value. At the same time, you ignore people you do not value. In effect, by ignoring them, you devalue them and make them feel less important.

Here is an example: Imagine being engaged in a pleasant conversation with another person face to face. But then, as the other person is speaking, you simply look away and stop listening. How would the other person feel? How would you feel if somebody turned away and stopped listening to you in the middle of a conversation?

The more closely you pay attention to another person, the more valuable and important he feels. As a result, he likes and trusts you, and enjoys being with you. Paying attention to another person is the fastest way to satisfy his deep emotional need to feel important and to make him feel happy about himself.

THE BENEFIT OF SUCCESS
■

Some years ago, I found myself sitting next to a businessman on a flight from San Diego to Chicago. He turned out to be a wealthy and successful executive who had started and built a $300 million company. During that flight, he told me a story that I never forgot.

He said that he had just been at a three-day meeting in San Diego with several other top executives, a meeting that ended with a long pleasant dinner at an expensive restaurant.

All of these men had started with little or nothing and had become successful over the years. As they were talking about and sharing their successes, one member of the group spoke up and asked, "What is success?"

Since this man was one of the smartest and most insightful people at the table, everyone quieted down to listen to his answer to his question. He then said, "Success means no more difficult people in your life." (He actually used another, more colorful word to refer to difficult people. Use your imagination.)

A SIMPLE TRUTH
■

Everyone laughed and agreed. They all realized that one of the greatest blessings of success, especially financial success, is that you can decide not to have anything to do with negative people, for any reason. You do not have to allow them into your life, and if they are already there, you can get them out of your life. You can decide to live and work only with people who you like, respect, and enjoy.

Here is the question: Why do you allow negative people to be in your life in the first place? Negative people are the primary source of almost all of your unhappiness. They cause you more pain, anger, frustration, aggravation, and unhappiness than all other factors put together. Why do you allow them in your life in the first place?

The answer is usually because you think that the rewards or benefits you will eventually receive from your relationship with this negative person will be greater than the costs, pain, and aggravation that you will suffer by putting up with her.

But here is the point: Did you ever get anything good or beneficial from continuing to associate with a negative or difficult person? And the answer is always no. No matter how long you put up with the negative person, at the end of the day, you received no lasting benefit whatsoever. In fact, the opposite was probably true. The cost to you of that negative relationship was enormous, and there were never any off-setting benefits.

THE GREAT LESSON
∎

Here is the point: The wealthiest and most successful people have finally reached the point at which they refuse to have any negative people in their lives. But because having negative people in your life never brings you any advantage or benefit anyway, you can decide right now to do the same thing as the richest and most successful people in the world do. You can decide, this very minute, to get rid of all the negative people in your life.

Resolve this very moment that you are not going to have difficult people in your life. If they are there currently, you are going to get rid of them immediately. From now on, you are going to live and work only with people you like and enjoy. You decide right now that you will absolutely refuse to have anything to do with people who make you feel unhappy or negative in any way.

This is one of the most important and best decisions you will ever make. The very act of deciding to get rid of a particular negative person in your life will cause you to smile and feel happy. You will actually feel a sense of a relief even before you have done anything to end the negative situation.

Is there anyone in your life who, knowing what you now know, you would not invite back into your life again today, if you had to do it over? This is one of the most important questions that you'll ever ask and answer for yourself.

People and family times are easily the most important times of your life. The way you deal with these times day by day and even minute by minute has more of an effect on your happiness and success than any other factor.

<<< ACTION EXERCISES >>>

1. Identify the most important people in your life, those people whose health, happiness, and self-esteem are key concerns of yours.

2. Decide on the most important things you could say or do to make them feel happier and more valuable.

3. Resolve today to do or say something every day to someone for the express purpose of making him or her feel more valuable and important.

9

REST AND RELAXATION TIME

Deep within man dwell those slumbering powers; powers that would astonish him, that he never dreamed of possessing; forces that would revolutionize his life if aroused and put into action.

—ORISON SWETT MARDEN

All types of time, all minutes and hours, are not the same. As you have realized by now, there is a big difference between goal-setting time, creative time, and people time. There is also a big difference between work time and the time you spend in rest and recuperation.

Just as productive time requires intense focus and concentration on the most valuable use of your time at that moment, rest and relaxation time requires that you back off and do nothing productive or important at all.

It turns out that rich people, people who start with little or nothing and become wealthy over the course of their careers, sleep longer and take more time off than average people or poor people. You should also take more time off to rest and recharge your mental batteries as well.

THE NATURE OF KNOWLEDGE WORK

■

You are a knowledge worker. You work with your mind, your brain. You are not a factory or agricultural worker, working with your muscles, making and moving things to earn your living. The quality of your life is largely determined by the quality of your thinking.

The most valuable asset you bring to your business and your career is *rested thinking time*. This happens when you take enough time off so that you can think calmly and clearly, make good decisions, and do excellent work both for yourself and with others.

Your company has hired your brain and what you can do with that brain. Your job, your responsibility, is to ensure that you bring a rested, refreshed, alert, and sharp brain to work to focus on getting the results that are required of you.

Many people think that whether they are fully rested or not doesn't really matter. They think that it is the number of hours that they put in at work rather than the quality of those hours. But this is not true. Numerous studies have shown that after eight hours of work, your thinking ability begins to decline. After ten hours, you are functioning at about 50 percent of capacity. You are like a boxer during the last rounds of a fight, staying on your feet and slugging away, even though you are making little progress.

YOUR BRAIN AS A BATTERY
■

Think of your body as a vehicle that carries your brain around, and to and from work. You need a fully rested body to carry a fully rested and refreshed brain to work so that you can perform at your best.

Think of your brain like a battery, which loses its energy, discharges, and burns out over time. It is estimated that fully 80 percent of your energy is burned up by mental activity rather than physical activity. This is why at the end of a long business day or after an intense meeting, you can feel tired out, even exhausted, and hardly capable of deciding what you want for dinner. Your glucose, the energy that your brain runs on, is largely depleted.

Just like a cell phone needs to be recharged regularly so that it operates at its highest capability, you need to recharge your brain regularly as well. You need to set aside specific times, and often extended periods of time, to fully recharge your brain battery so that you can be alert and aware most of the time.

THE DANGER OF DOPAMINE
∎

As I mentioned earlier, we live today in the age of electronic distractions. If you do not control the world around you, you will find yourself bombarded with e-mails, texts, and telephone calls all day long. Each time you respond to the novelty or newness of an e-mail or a text message, your body releases a shot of dopamine, the same chemical found in cocaine. This dopamine acts as a stimulant and actually gives you a small feeling of pleasure.

This stimulus and feeling of pleasure motivate you to repeat the process, to respond to the next text or e-mail or to send a new e-mail or text to someone else. Once you answer your first e-mail in the morning, and get your first jolt of dopamine, you find it harder and harder not to respond to incoming messages, and eventually, you cannot resist at all.

Once you check your first e-mail or respond to the first text, you find yourself reacting and responding to electronic stimuli all day long. Recent research suggests that the sound of an incoming e-mail is similar to the sound of a slot machine bell ringing and coins falling. You immediately become curious to see what you just won. This is why you must *leave the thing off* if you are going to totally relax.

Taking care of your mental and physical health, your "machine," is essential and perhaps more important than anything else to ensure your health, happiness, and long-term success.

Your health and well-being are more important to the quality of your life than any other factors. To perform at your best, rest is essential. You need long periods of complete rest and relaxation when you do absolutely nothing but recharge your mental, physical, and emotional batteries.

Vince Lombardi once said, "Fatigue makes cowards of us all." When you are tired out, burned out, you are susceptible to stress and negativity, are likely to become angry and impatient, and may make choices and decisions that are not in your best long-term interests.

SET REST AS A PRIORITY
■

Sometimes, the very best use of your time is to come home and go to bed early, at 8:00 or 9:00 P.M., and just sleep for nine or ten hours, completely recharging your mental and physical batteries.

When you have a lot going on in your life, when you have important decisions and choices to make, sometimes the best advice is to sleep on it. Put off any important decision until you are fully rested.

Many years ago, my mentor, a successful business executive, gave me a little pamphlet called "Take Time Out for Mental Digestion." In this pamphlet, which I never forgot, the author recommended that you take seventy-two hours to think about a major choice or decision before taking action. This turns out to be a success secret of many top executives.

The more time you take to consider an important decision, the better quality decision you will make. This is because you get a chance to rest, to sleep on it, to turn it over in your mind, and to carefully consider all the ramifications of the decision.

SLOW DOWN TO GO FASTER

Most people feel that they have too much to do and too little time. They don't have time for all this rest we are recommending. They feel that they have to get up and get going early in the morning and work hard all day long, sometimes bringing work home in the evening and continuing to work until just before they go to bed. But this is false.

There is the story about the little girl who goes to her

mother and asks, "Mommy, why does Daddy bring a briefcase full of work home every night, and works all the time, and never spends time with the family?"

The mother gently answers her by saying, "Well, honey. You have to understand, Daddy has too much work to do at work so he has to bring it home in order to catch up."

The little girl says, "Mommy, why don't they just put him in a *slower* class?"

Be careful that you don't get put into a slower class as the result of being perceived as someone who is overwhelmed and unable to stay on top of her work.

VIOLATE PARKINSON'S LAW
■

The primary reason people have too much to do and too little time is because the average person is wasting fully 50 percent of her time at work in idle conversation, checking e-mail, taking long lunches and coffee breaks, and generally engaging in other nonwork activities. That is why one of the greatest success principles of all is to work all the time you work.

C. Northcote Parkinson, a British historian, wrote a book many years ago called *Parkinson's Law*. In this book, he made the famous observation that "Work expands to fill the time allotted for it." If you have eight hours to accomplish a certain number of tasks, you will take a full eight hours, and you will probably be rushing at the end of the day to finish your work.

But the reverse of Parkinson's Law is that "Work contracts to fill the time allotted for it." This means that if you give yourself a tighter deadline to get all your work done, you will work faster and more efficiently and sometimes accomplish even a full day's work in just a couple of hours.

SET DEADLINES ON YOURSELF
■

One of my seminar attendees, a successful business-man, told me an interesting story. He said that when he got married he promised his wife that he would be home by 6:00 each night and would spend at least two solid hours with her every single day and more on the weekends. When his children were born, he expanded that to three hours per day and more time on the weekends. He told me that if he had to be out of town, he would religiously make up the lost hours by spending even more time with his wife and his children.

He said that this promise, made early in his career, changed his life. To keep his promise, he disciplined himself to work efficiently and on his most important tasks, all day long. He went to work a little earlier, worked a little harder, and finished up in time to be home with his family for dinner by 6:00. He became one of the most productive executives in his industry; was paid more and promoted rapidly; and over the course of his career, became quite wealthy. He said that making that promise to his wife was one of the most important things he ever did.

You can do the same. Remember, it is not the number of hours that you put in but the amount that you produce in those hours. To produce the best quality and quantity of work requires that you be fully rested every working hour of every day. You owe this to yourself and to your company.

OBSERVE THE SABBATH

■

Orthodox Jews honor the Sabbath in a particular way as an important part of their religious practice. From sundown on Friday to sundown on Saturday, they refrain from all work of any kind. They take a full twenty-four hours during which they engage in religious and family activities.

This is a wonderful concept that I adapted to my life many years ago and which many of my students have incorporated as well. Each week, discipline yourself to take off at least one full day where you do no business work at all. What you need is two full nights of rest, with no work in between.

One good night's rest does not seem to be enough. What you need is to sleep deeply and well on one night, completely relax and refresh for a full day, and then get another full night's sleep. This one day, two-night combination recharges your mental and physical batteries. By the end of these thirty-six hours, you will be sharper, more alert, and more creative. You will be happier and more positive. Your personality will improve. You will be a better husband, wife, mate, or friend and will be more enjoyable to be around. It is amazing what rest will do.

ALLOW NO EXCEPTIONS
∎

During this thirty-six-hour period, you must discipline yourself to turn off your computer, to refuse to do any work at all, even reading through papers or work from the office or answering lengthy business e-mails on your phone. Just stop. Refuse to do anything that requires concentration or mental energy.

Here is what happens: If you interrupt your day off by doing just a little paperwork, it is like jerking the plug out of the socket. The recharging process stops. You stop resting. By not allowing yourself a full day of uninterrupted time, your mental batteries do not become fully recharged. By interrupting your rest, you end up not getting very much rest at all.

How often have you returned from a vacation more tired than when you left? It was because you kept pecking away at your work the whole time.

At first, you will find this idea of stopping work completely for thirty-six hours to be quite difficult. This is because you may feel you are on a treadmill. No matter how much you get done, you are convinced that there is always more to do. Even worse, if you are doing work that you enjoy and getting results that are important to you, it is normal, natural, and easy for your work to spill out into your evenings and over into your weekends. It often takes more discipline to stop working than it does to continue working.

A TEST OF CHARACTER
■

Think of this as a test of character. If you don't deliberately interrupt this style of working, seven days a week, you soon fall into the trap of working most of the time. You find yourself continually checking your e-mail, replying to texts, and initiating new work activities, always being plugged in and connected. You become like that horse pulling the wheel around in a circle all day long, never stopping.

But the key to your real success, to high levels of productivity and performance, is for you to disconnect completely for extended periods of time. Turn off your computer and refuse to restart it or check it for at least thirty-six hours each week. Check your smartphone if you want, but discipline yourself to postpone any responses during your rest time.

The best news is that instead of falling behind in your work, once you have fully recharged mentally and physically, you will get more work done of higher quality in the next two or three hours than you might have done in an entire day of working while mentally and emotionally fatigued. You will usually have your best ideas and breakthroughs after a relaxed weekend or extended vacation.

DO WHAT RICH PEOPLE DO
■

You read of wealthy people who take extended vacations to beautiful resorts all over the world. You get brochures offering luxury vacations on cruise ships.

You may have wondered how these people can take so many vacations and be so wealthy at the same time.

The answer is simple. They place a high premium on recharging their batteries. In addition, they almost always take their vacations with other successful people. During their periods of rest and relaxation, they socialize and chat about what they are doing in their work, about business opportunities and possibilities, new breakthroughs and inventions, and so on. When they come back from these vacations fully rested, their minds are sparkling with new ideas and insights that they can use to make even more money in the future.

SLEEP DEPRIVATION HURTS YOU
■

Meanwhile, people of average income and most poor people burn the candle at both ends. They may work long hours, but when they come home, they watch television for five to seven hours each evening. They go to bed only when they are too tired to watch television. They sleep for six or seven hours, and the first thing they do when they wake up is turn on the television again.

Most people in our society, almost 70 percent, are suffering from sleep deprivation. This is an insidious problem. Instead of getting a full eight or nine hours of sleep each night, the recommended minimum to fully recharge your mental and physical abilities, most people try to get by on six or seven hours, sometimes less, especially if they don't sleep well.

As a result, they build up an accumulating sleep deficit of one or two hours each night. As the week goes on, these individuals become more and more tired. They have less and less mental energy. At work, they just go through the motions, consuming copious quantities of coffee and caffeine-laced soft drinks to stay awake. They engage in endless conversations with co-workers because these conversations require very little thought. They eat too much because their bodies need the extra energy. They drink too much in the evening because they are burned out and need the sugar energy they get from alcohol. They seldom perform at high levels or reach their potential. They are simply too tired most of the time.

CHANGE YOUR LIFE

One of my clients was quite successful, running his own business. But he told me that he was not enjoying his work very much anymore, and he was tired most of the time. He was also overweight. He was eating and drinking too much.

I asked him how many hours he was sleeping each night. He told me that he was forcing himself to sleep only five or six hours per night so that he could have more work time. I told him that he was putting himself on an endless treadmill, working longer and longer hours, becoming more and more tired, accomplishing less and less, and losing his enthusiasm for work. I suggested that he discipline himself from now on to go to bed by 10:00 P.M. and sleep at least eight hours each night.

This was a novel idea for him. He had convinced himself that successful people slept less and worked longer hours. But he followed my advice. At our next coaching meeting, ninety days later, he told me that he had disciplined himself to start going to bed early and sleeping a full eight hours every night. He said that after a week, he felt as if he were waking up from a deep slumber, emerging from a fog.

He had no idea how tired he had become. But as he slept eight to nine hours each night, he had more and more energy. As a result, he ate less because he no longer required more food energy to keep him going during the day. He lost sixteen pounds in ninety days.

He said that going to bed early had changed his entire

life. Over the course of the next year, he tripled his income as well. He spent more time at home, took weekends off, took long vacations with his family, and made more money than he had ever dreamed of. He lost more and more weight and eventually got down to his ideal weight.

GUARANTEE YOUR VACATIONS
∎

Here is something you can do to guarantee that you don't slip back into working on weekends and during vacations. Promise others—your spouse, children, family, and friends—that you are going to dedicate a full day every weekend to them, to do what they want to do. Once you promise others and make the commitment to spend the time with them, you will seldom go back on your word.

Promise yourself that you will pull the plug on busy work and instead just relax on your days of rest and relaxation. You can read the paper, watch television, go for a walk or engage in other physical exercise, go to a movie, go out to dinner, or visit your friends, but you must refuse to do any work of any kind at all. Use your amazing mind to keep yourself active all day without doing any heavy mental lifting, any brainwork.

You have heard it said that a change is as good as a rest. This is based on research showing that you actually have three forms of energy—mental, emotional, and physical. If you burn out your mental energy during the course of the week in doing your work, you can recharge your brain over the weekend by switching to physical activities. In this way, you give your mental energies a chance to rejuvenate.

If you are going through an emotionally draining situation, be sure to get more sleep. Try to take a complete break by engaging in a physical activity, even going for a walk, to give yourself a chance to recharge.

MAKE R & R A WAY OF LIFE
■

In addition to taking one full day off each week, when you do no mental work at all, you should plan to take a three-day vacation every couple of months with your spouse or mate. But to get the maximum benefit out of these short vacations, you need to get two full nights of sleep when you are away.

I live in San Diego. My wife and I often drive to Palm Springs, a two-and-a-half-hour drive, for a three-day weekend, leaving on Friday and coming back on Sunday afternoon. Sometimes, we will fly to San Francisco on the same schedule and spend two full days in a hotel, going out for dinner, and just relaxing. These turn out to be some of the most enjoyable times of our lives.

In addition, set a goal to take two, three, or four weeks away on vacation each year. During this time, you may occasionally check your e-mail to make sure there are no emergencies, but generally speaking you leave things off.

If you are living and working intensely, you will require three or four or even five days on vacation to decompress and to start to fully relax. Up to that time, you will still be mentally running on the treadmill, thinking about your work and things that you could do while you are gone.

During this period of decompression, you must discipline yourself to keep busy doing things other than work. Turn your computer off. Get out and move around. Go for walks. Go out for dinner. Go sightseeing. But don't do any work until the compulsion to work eventually dies away, which it will.

FAMILY VACATIONS
∎

This idea of long vacations does not always come easy. I was in my late thirties before I first took a two-week vacation, and I felt guilty about not working the whole time. But in the long run, I really enjoyed the experience.

The next year, we took another long vacation, and we have taken long vacations every year ever since. At the beginning, it took me at least three days before I could get off the mental treadmill and stop thinking about the work I had left behind. Today, with the passing of time and with the increased busyness of my schedule, it takes me a full week to come down. Until then, I have to fight the irresistible desire to open up my laptop and communicate with the rest of the world. This may happen to you as well.

Remember, the more you take time off—daily, weekly, monthly, and annually—to allow yourself to rest completely, the more productive you will be when you go back to work. Sometimes, you will have one great idea while you are on vacation that may save you a year or even five years of hard work. But you have to create the rested time for this inspiration to occur.

PLAN VACATIONS IN ADVANCE
■

There is a great technique that has been a life-changer for me for more than three decades. It is this: Each

January, plan your time off and vacation calendar for the year to come. Mark off the days you will take off each week, your two- and three-day getaways, and your one- and two-week vacations. Then call and book your vacations with a nonrefundable deposit. Once you have paid a nonrefundable deposit, you are committed. You will very seldom ever miss a vacation for which you have prepaid.

My wife and I go to Hawaii for three weeks at Christmas each year with our family. The complex where we stay is very popular and is fully booked throughout December and January. Because of this, they require a deposit on January 5 to hold the condominium that you want to stay in, half payment by April 1, and full payment by June 1. And the payments are nonrefundable. In thirty years, we have never failed to take these family vacations. We have never missed a day. It will be the same with you.

Rest and recreation time is some of the most important time of your life. Many of your best ideas, ideas that can make you successful and even wealthy, will come to you after a period of complete physical and mental vacation. Carving out blocks of time where you can totally relax is one of the most important and valuable uses of your time and can make all the difference in your life and your future.

<<< ACTION EXERCISES >>>

1. Resolve today that you are going to build a rest and relaxation schedule into your life to ensure you will perform at your best in your work.

2. Plan your vacation schedule at the beginning of the year, and then plan your work responsibilities around it.

3. Book and pay for your vacations early in the year to ensure you never delay or procrastinate on the rest and relaxation you need.

QUIET TIME

Dream lofty dreams, and as you
dream, so shall you become. Your
vision is the promise of what you
shall one day be; your ideal is the
prophecy of what you shall at
last unveil.

—JAMES ALLEN

The time that you spend alone with yourself in silence can be some of the most important time of your life. This special kind of time embraces spiritual development, mindfulness, contemplation, solitude, and meditation. The regular practice of these disciplines will change your life in a most amazing way.

SPIRITUAL DEVELOPMENT

■

The highest human ideal is and has always been the achievement of *inner peace*. The true measure of how well you are doing in your life can be determined by what percentage of the time you feel at peace with yourself and others.

Throughout history, people have developed different religious and spiritual traditions of all kinds, all over the world. In every case, these people were seeking something higher and greater than themselves, some supreme set of values or beliefs to which they could aspire. The ultimate aim of these religious traditions is to help guide and direct people toward higher levels of well-being, happiness, and inner peace.

Spiritual development can bring you more peace and joy than perhaps any other activity. Spiritual development requires, among other things, that you practice *mindfulness* on a regular basis. In its simplest terms, mindfulness is that state you enter into when you discipline yourself to become completely quiet and aware of yourself and your environment.

THE WORK OF SPIRITUAL DEVELOPMENT
∎

Spiritual development requires a combination of learning accompanied by reflection on how you could apply these ideas to your life.

Aristotle wrote, "Wisdom is an equal combination of experience plus reflection." Constant busyness, electronic interruptions, television, and socializing all keep our minds so busy that we seldom have time to actually stop and think about what we are doing or what is really happening around us.

When you are so busy that you don't take time to

reflect on the experiences of your life, you don't learn, grow, and develop the wisdom that you need to be a fully mature, fully functioning person.

The more time you take to think and reflect on your experiences, the deeper will be your knowledge and intelligence. As a result, you will find yourself making better decisions and fewer mistakes.

Mindfulness requires that you discipline yourself to stop and think on a regular basis about what you are doing, and how you are doing it. Fortunately, you can practice this mindfulness at any time by simply slowing down.

MINDFULNESS MADE SIMPLE
∎

A simple technique for mindfulness, for centering, for calming your mind completely, is called *stopping thoughts.*

Your ability to stop your thoughts, to clear your mind, requires that you shift your focus and attention away from your day-to-day life and onto something as simple as breathing in and breathing out.

Because you can think only one thought at a time, when you think about your breathing, you automatically stop thinking about anything else, especially something that might cause you anger or stress at the moment.

When you can get your mind busy elsewhere, thinking about something else, or nothing at all, this shuts out any negativity in your life. The negative events or thoughts gradually begin to subside in importance. Sometimes they disappear altogether, like cigarette smoke in a large room.

A breathing technique that you can use to stop thoughts, to calm your mind, and to increase your level of mindfulness is to sit quietly with your hands in your lap, not touching, and then inhale to the count of seven. Take deep, deep breaths, inhaling as deeply as you possibly can. Count to seven as you do this.

Then hold your breath to the slow count of seven. Finally, exhale your breath to the count of seven. Do this complete exercise seven times whenever you are experiencing stress or anger, or in advance of an important event, like a meeting or presentation.

This 7-7-7 Method of breathing will trigger the release of endorphins in your brain. Endorphins are called nature's happy drug. A tiny amount of these hormones will give you a feeling of peace and a sense of mental clarity. You will be more happy and creative.

REMEMBER YOURSELF

■

The metaphysician Pyotr Ouspensky taught the practice of "self-remembering" as a way of centering oneself and increasing self-awareness. Ouspensky taught that we have hundreds and thousands of thoughts that flow through our mind in an endless stream-of-consciousness, like a river. This never-ending flow of thoughts causes us to fall into a form of "waking sleep" in which we function almost automatically and often unaware of our surroundings.

Everyone has had the experience of getting into their car and driving to work and not remembering a single thing about the trip. Your mind was so lost in thought that you drove to your office on autopilot, without thinking, because you had driven the route so many times before.

It is only when something happens unexpectedly, like hitting a patch of ice or almost having an accident, that you suddenly wake up. At that moment, you become completely aware of yourself and your surroundings. But as soon as the moment passes, you once more go back to waking sleep.

In the New Testament Jesus says, "Awake, all ye who sleep." This was meant to encourage people to be more thoughtful and aware, to pay closer attention to the meaning of what he was saying rather than reacting automatically, which is the normal way that most people process information.

To experience mindfulness and self-remembering, simply say the words *I am here*. As you say these words, look around you as if you were seeing your world and surroundings for the first time. Notice the details of all the things around you. Imagine describing your surroundings to a blind person or to a person on the phone, who has never seen or experienced your environment. When you do this, you see far more, and become more sensitive to your world than you were before.

MINDFULNESS DURING REGULAR LIFE
■

Most people eat quickly, unthinkingly. They pay little attention to their food or surroundings. But you can turn dining into a mindful experience. While you are eating, you can slow down and observe all the details involved in the dining experience, and the various features of the room. Become aware of your environment. Look at the way the table is set, at the dishes, cutlery, and glasses.

As you eat, chew slowly, thoughtfully, and deliberately. Take the time to chew your food thoroughly, savoring the different tastes, and enjoying each small bite. Notice the flavors, the smells, the different tastes of the food, as though you were eating this food for the first time or for the last time.

You can dramatically increase your mindfulness by simply slowing down a regular activity and observing yourself as you move. For example, if you simply slow down the speed of your walking, you become immediately aware of your movements. You actually "remember yourself" better. You become more conscious of yourself and the world around you. You think, "I am here."

When you slow down any activity, like washing the dishes, brushing your teeth, or even turning the pages of the newspaper, you immediately experience a heightened awareness of your actions and become much more sensitive to your environment.

PRACTICING MINDFULNESS FOR PROBLEM SOLVING
■

Whenever you have a problem of any kind, practice *solitude*. Go into the silence to find the solution. Sit down comfortably in a place where there is no noise or distractions. Let your mind relax completely.

Prepare to spend twenty-five to thirty minutes of silent sitting before your mind stops racing and thinking about the things that are going on in your daily life. At about the thirty-minute point of complete silence, your mind will become completely calm and you will begin to feel an amazing sense of peace. You will start to see things with greater clarity. And while you are sitting there quietly, in silence, the exact answer to your most important question or problem will simply appear in your mind.

Because sitting in the silence stimulates superconscious activity, when the answer to your problem or question comes to you, it will be simple and clear. It will answer every detail of the problem or difficulty. It will be completely within your capacity to implement immediately.

Each time you practice solitude, the still, small voice within will speak to you with greater clarity. Over time, this quiet voice actually becomes louder, and more insistent. It functions faster and with greater accuracy. This development of your intuitive sense is one of the best uses of time of all and is the key to spiritual development.

THINK ABOUT WATER
∎

Another way for you to trigger your superconscious powers, and to develop yourself to higher levels of spirituality, is for you to think about water. Because the human body is 70 percent water, we have a natural affinity for water of all kinds, especially bodies of water. Whenever you sit quietly next to a body of water, your mind soon becomes calm and clear, and your intuitive senses begins to flow, like a river.

If you are not near water, you can just think about a body of water. Think about a lake or the ocean or even a quiet stream where the water babbles along in front of you. Thinking about water in this way relaxes your mind and stimulates ideas and insights into your current situation.

Even sitting by a swimming pool, in the silence, gazing out at the water before you, has a calming effect on your mind and emotions.

THE PRACTICE OF MEDITATION
∎

Meditation is practiced by millions of people all over the world on a daily basis, and sometimes several times a day.

In meditation, you sit in the silence with your eyes closed and breathe deeply, in and out, focusing your attention on your diaphragm, the place where your lungs meet your stomach.

Many meditators use a mantra, a simple word or phrase such as *peace, love,* or *serenity,* which they repeat over and over until they fall into a relaxed state of harmony and bliss.

Often meditators will sit in front of a candle in a darkened, quiet room concentrating on their breathing for twenty to sixty minutes. There is even an app that shows a burning candle that you can sit and look at to help your meditation.

Another method of mental relaxation is called "walking meditation," which is best done in nature, by yourself. You can walk around your neighborhood or nearby park. You can walk in the woods or along the beach. You will enjoy the same benefits of relaxation and enhanced creativity as you would sitting quietly by yourself.

As it happens, not all people can meditate. Some people prefer sitting still and looking outward, with no disturbances or interruptions. This is called *contemplation,* sitting with your eyes open and simply allowing your mind to float freely without any attempt to control your thoughts. Either meditation or contemplation will work for you in bringing you the peace you seek or the solutions you are looking for.

THE BIG PAYOFF
■

The French writer Pascal said, "All the problems of the human race stem from man's inability to sit quietly by himself in a room."

When you include periods of mindfulness, solitude, meditation, and contemplation in your life, you will feel happier, healthier, and more in control of yourself and your emotions.

The good news is that meditation, contemplation, and solitude are purely beneficial acts. Each of them lowers your flash point, reduces your stress, and makes you more relaxed and resilient in the face of day-to-day problems.

People report extraordinary benefits from mindful living, enjoying greater clarity and alertness, a heightened sense of self-control, and greater personal power. They experience lower blood pressure, less stress, better sleep, superior health, and many other good things, including weight loss.

Resolve right now that you are going to take a few minutes each day, perhaps just five minutes at the beginning, to sit perfectly still, quietly, with no distractions and just let your mind float peacefully. Think about your breathing or think about water. From the first time you practice this mindfulness, you will be more alert and aware and feel better about yourself and your world.

<<< ACTION EXERCISES >>>

1. Go into the silence on a regular basis, once per day if possible. Practice solitude to tune into your higher powers.
2. Practice mindfulness, slowing down to increase your sense of awareness, when you eat, work, and talk with others.
3. Practice meditation for a few minutes each day by closing your eyes while you sit peacefully and let your mind flow like a quiet stream.

SUMMARY

The most valuable and important thing you do is to think. The quality of your thinking, especially about time, determines the quality of your life. Continually stop and ask, What is the most appropriate type of time for me to use in this situation?

When you take the time to think before you react or respond, you will always make better decisions and get better results.

Good luck!

—Brian Tracy

ALSO FROM

Brian Tracy

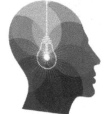

How to Think and Act Like the
Most Successful and Highest-Paid
People in Every Field

Brian Tracy

Bestselling author of *Eat That Frog!*

tarcherperigee